A DEAL WITH THE DEVIL

The Green Party in Government

Mary Minihan

Published in 2011 by MAVERICK HOUSE PUBLISHERS, Office 19, Dunboyne
Business Park, Dunboyne, Co. Meath, Ireland.

info@maverickhouse.com
http://www.maverickhouse.com

ISBN: 978-1-905379-75-0

5 4 3 2 1

The paper used in this book comes from wood pulp of managed forests. For every
tree felled, at least one tree is planted, thereby renewing natural resources.

A CIP catalogue record for this book is available from the British Library.

DEDICATION

For Eoin Minihan

Acknowledgements

Sincere thanks are due to many people who are or have been connected to the Green Party and who spoke to me both on and off the record in the course of my research.

Thanks to political correspondents Harry McGee and Deaglán de Bréadún, who have written extensively and knowledgeably on the Greens, along with former political correspondents Mark Hennessy and Miriam Donohoe.

With particular thanks also to Stephen Collins, political editor of *The Irish Times*, for his advice, support and encouragement throughout the period of writing this book. A debt of gratitude is also due to all my journalistic colleagues and friends in Leinster House, who contribute towards making it such an enjoyable place to work.

CONTENTS

Chapter 1

Gormley's asylum

"It has been stated by deputies on the other side that the Opposition has been placed in a straitjacket. That is an apt analogy in more ways than one. I warn those other parties that they should know when they enter government during this crisis, they will be entering an asylum."

On the last day of November 2010, almost three-and-a-half years into his party's first ever period in government, John Gormley, the then leader of the Green Party, a glass-half-empty kind of man at the best of times, was stressed out and pessimistic about Ireland's future. In an extraordinary, angst-ridden contribution to a Dáil debate on a controversial deal just agreed with the International Monetary Fund (IMF), Gormley admitted to being eaten up inside by the economic decisions which the Fianna Fáil/Green Government was being forced to make following Ireland's loss of economic sovereignty.

Gormley was clearly frazzled. Once an advocate of early nights with plenty of sleep, he was now suffering from stress-induced insomnia and certain his party was facing electoral wipeout. He addressed his pointed comments to the Opposition benches, where sat the Labour Party leader Eamon Gilmore. Power was by this stage well within Gilmore's grasp, and within a few short months he would become Tánaiste to Fine Gael leader Enda Kenny's Taoiseach in a new coalition government.

Gormley warned Gilmore that soon he too would "have to endure the sleepless nights, the no-win situation and the non-stop criticism."

Sinn Féin TDs in particular would attack Gilmore non-stop, Gormley predicted, correctly, but the Labour leader would have no choice but to pursue the harsh economic policies that were being locked into place by the powerful troika of the IMF, European Union (EU) and European Central Bank (ECB).

"All Deputy Gilmore will be able to say in reply, just as we have said, is that he has no choice but to act," Gormley continued.

"There is nothing worse in a democracy when a politician must act in a way because his or her choices are limited. Deputy Gilmore will be faced with that lack of choice which will eat him up inside."

At the height of another crisis just a few short years earlier, Gormley's mobile phone had bleeped to announce the arrival of a text message from Mary Harney, the wily politician who led the Progressive Democrats and at the time was the government's minister for health. "The worst day in government is better than the best day in Opposition," her message read. The intervention, meant to steady Gormley's nerves, worked for a while. But if he agreed with Harney's assessment at that time, when the Government was facing a so-called 'grey power' uprising from elderly people opposed to budgetary changes restricting access to medical cards for the over-70s, he clearly did not do so by the end of 2010.

Shortly after the Green leader's overwrought outburst in the Dáil chamber, all six Green TDs would dramatically lose their seats in the game-changing General Election of February 2011, which drastically altered the parliamentary representation of political parties in Ireland – perhaps for good.

Gormley had been a cabinet minister, holding the environment brief. The portfolio had been long coveted by his party, but Gormley's time there was dominated towards the end of his term by bizarre and unexpected tangles with Fianna Fáil backbenchers over stag-hunting and dog-breeding legislation. This was much to the dismay of many urban Greens, some of whom would barely have been able to distinguish one end of a hunting dog from the other.

There was undoubtedly a disproportionate southside Dublin, middle-class element to the party's elected membership, which the party would pay dearly for. Outside the capital, dislike of Gormley in particular reached fever-pitch in the run-up to the election, with pro-hunting campaigners denouncing him as "a fella on a bicycle in Dublin telling you how to run a farm." Although inclined to a negative reading of political runes, and given indeed to some moments of darkness, Gormley's strategic instincts were probably better than any of his party colleagues.

He wanted to pull out of Government much earlier than any other Green, but was repeatedly over-ruled. This state of affairs naturally frustrated Gormley, and yet he accepted it. It remains most unusual in Irish politics for a leader to be so regularly undermined, and observers struggled to understand the Green approach to the concept of consensual and collegiate leadership, which was far removed from the *uno duce, una voce* approach traditionally adopted by other Irish political parties.

Gormley's only Cabinet colleague in the small party was Eamon Ryan, an optimist and a skilled communicator whose manner sometimes strayed past the passionate and visionary and towards the evangelical. The photogenic Ryan had briefly entertained ambitions to run for the Presidency in 2004, but in the end did not seek a nomination to run against the incumbent Mary McAleese, citing a lack of resources and difficulties in obtaining the backing of 20 b representatives required for a nomination. In the immediate aftermath of his aborted bid he admitted he had acted rashly, but later said it had been the right thing to attempt.

Ryan relished the challenge of heading up his Department of Communications, Energy and Natural Resources from 2007 onwards, having followed the area with genuine interest for many years. Until the very end, he argued that the Greens should stay in Government for as long as they could for legacy and policy reasons: in order to attempt to have as much of their agenda implemented as possible. Ryan rarely attracted the level of anger that Gormley inspired, thanks in part to his ability to deflect criticism, resist engaging in unwinnable arguments and keep talking about policy in interviews and media appearances – no matter what the question had been. He would go on to take up the leadership of the shell-shocked party after the devastating 2011 General Election.

The delicately balanced relationship between Ryan and Gormley was central to most of the party's failures and successes in power. The pair already knew each other inside out by the time they became Cabinet Ministers. When Gormley, who was born in 1959, contested his first Dáil election in 1989, Ryan, four years his junior, was his election agent. Gormley handed his Dublin City Council seat to Ryan the year after he eventually became a TD for Dublin South-East in 1997, and Ryan, representing Dublin South, followed Gormley into the Dáil in 2002. Although they cleverly maintained the outward appearance of an united front throughout their time in Government, they were an odd couple whose relationship was not always perfectly harmonious. Their innate personality differences meant they were often at odds when it came to both strategy and style. Ryan, who seemed to wake up happy every day, was a conflict-avoider; Gormley was a fretter who did not shirk from a good row. Close observers within the party maintained that the pair simply did not talk enough and failed to co-ordinate their approach to Cabinet discussions adequately.

Although Gormley and Ryan certainly kept things civilised, personnel in their respective camps would occasionally reveal a sometimes amusing clash of cultures. Environmentally-friendly travel arrangements for a work trip abroad were being casually discussed between Gormley and a key aide in the Dáil canteen one afternoon. "How would Eamon cross the water?" Gormley wondered aloud. "Oh, he's walking," came the tongue-in-cheek response.

Trevor Sargent had been a TD since 1992, the year the party's first ever deputy Roger Garland failed to be re-elected. Sargent became the Green's first leader in 2001. The party had held out against the concept of leadership for more than two decades on theoretical grounds, quaintly fearing that a cult of personality could emerge to destroy the cherished, if laborious, tradition of grassroots decision making. Such a situation was unlikely to ever occur with the modest and mild-mannered Sargent at the helm, however. Respected across party divides for his integrity, he consolidated his image as the whiter-than-white ethical conscience of the Green Party in 1993, when he was famously caught in a headlock by an apoplectic Don Lydon of Fianna Fáil during a council meeting. Sargent had been waving a cheque for £100 and asking other Dublin councillors if they had also received one from a developer in order to assist their decision making when it came to a rezoning vote. Lydon later dismissed his hands-on involvement in the incident as nothing but a bit of "divilment."

Just a year younger than Gormley, Sargent was a member of the Church of Ireland who found prayer therapeutic at moments of worry. Devoted to his organic garden, he brought a sandwich with home-grown salads to work in the Dáil every day. Sargent had thrown himself into constituency work in Dublin North after standing down from his junior ministerial post amid some controversy in 2010. He held the one seat party activists thought could be salvaged in the following year's general election, but he too lost out.

So did Paul Gogarty, the unpredictable and sometimes outspoken Dublin Mid-West deputy who was the only Green TD from the class of 2007 not to eventually achieve some form of ministerial office. The youngest Green, born at the end of 1968, he was credited with holding the line against education cuts. Never publicity-shy, Gogarty is best remembered for directing a most unpleasant expletive towards an opponent in the course of an ugly debate in the Dáil chamber. He is also remembered for bringing his 18-month-old daughter Daisy, and her teddy bear, to a press conference at which the Green Party finally demanded a General Election.

Ciaran Cuffe was the inscrutable, urbane minister of state who had most clearly articulated the danger for the Greens of entering government with Fianna Fáil in 2007. It would be "a deal with the devil", he predicted. The reserved, quiet man of the party, he tended to express himself more forcefully online than he did in person. Born in 1963, the same year as Ryan, Cuffe longed for full ministerial office but it was not to be. A secret plan agreed in 2007 as the Greens entered Government, but subsequently abandoned, would have seen Cuffe rotated into the Cabinet in place of Gormley.

Cuffe always appeared to have very little chance of holding his seat in the highly competitive and crowded Dun Laoghaire constituency, which a political opponent dubbed "the group of death." He pushed for legislation which eventually gave effect to civil partnerships for same-sex couples, although he would have preferred the law to go further and allow for gay marriage. Cuffe criticised the endurance of dynasties in Irish politics, despite having a link to the most famous political family of them all: his mother's sister, Ethel, was married to Bobby Kennedy.

The Green's deputy leader Mary White, a Mills and Boon writer turned junior minister, represented Carlow-Kilkenny. Born in 1948, she was the party's only TD representing a constituency outside the wider Dublin area, as well as its sole female deputy. Along with Gormley, she bore the brunt of an intensive campaign against Green-sponsored legislative measures to ban stag-hunting with packs of dogs and to regulate dog-breeding establishments. Proponents of traditional rural sports dubbed her "a dangerous woman" and she was spat at in the street as the 2011 General Election approached and the political temperature soared. She kept up a cheery persona throughout the party's torrid time in Government but, despite being something of a Pollyanna in a sea of Cassandras, White's relentlessly positive nature was never going to save her seat.

Although outside the Green's small Dáil group, the party chairman and finance spokesman Senator Dan Boyle was also a central figure. Born in Chicago the year before Ryan and Cuffe, Boyle was a hyperactive Twitter user with an unlucky knack for rubbing people up the wrong way. He came to be viewed as an outrider who was granted leeway to express the unspoken views of the six party TDs on issues of sensitivity between the Coalition partners. Green press advisers continued to insist the rotund Corkman was operating in a personal capacity as he became more and more outspoken from the safe distance of cyberspace. Fianna Fáil representatives at first failed to understand and became increasingly infuriated by Boyle's busy use of the micro-blogging website, while some Green colleagues were also less than enthusiastic about the views he expressed online. Boyle had failed to retain his Cork South-Central Dáil seat in 2007 and was unsuccessful again in the constituency come 2011.

The Greens, having tasted national office just once, were completely wiped out as an electoral force on a country-wide scale by furious voters in one rural and five Dublin constituencies. Crucially, their electoral support fell to a minuscule 1.8 per cent, putting the party below the two per cent threshold required to continue receiving funding from the State. The curious thing was that when considering joining a Fianna Fáil-led administration almost four years earlier, many in the Greens plainly saw the danger of entering coalition with the larger, dominant party. Cuffe had prophesied that the "deal with the devil" would result in the party being "spat out" and "decimated." Yet the Greens chose to pass along the enchanted way into Government for the first time in the party's history. In Government, the often over-whelmed Greens would prove capable of making a great number of serious mistakes and naive misjudgments all by themselves, without any help whatsoever from Fianna Fáil.

A NIGHTMARE SCENARIO ALSO CAME TO PASS FOR THE SENIOR coalition partner. Fianna Fáil, until then the near-permanent party of power in the State, left the 30th Dáil with 72 TDs and limped back with just 20, while the greatly-regretted death of Brian Lenihan, the former Fianna Fáil finance minister just four months after the election would leave the party with zero representation in Dublin.

CHAPTER 2

PLANET BERTIE – 'A MARRIAGE OF PRAGMATISM AND IDEALISM'

FORMALLY ENTERING COALITION WITH FIANNA FÁIL IN JUNE 2007 meant the Greens had to plot a course for "Planet Bertie." John Gormley had coined the derisory nickname for the world inhabited by the Fianna Fáil leader as recently as February of that very same year.

"Planet Bertie" existed in a parallel universe where political gombeenism was the name of the game, Gormley suggested in the course of an ever-so-slightly wacky and soundbite-rich address to the Green's national convention in Galway. "On Planet Bertie, you can sign blank cheques, because everyone does it apparently. On Planet Bertie you can spend the average industrial wage on make-up. On Planet Bertie you can save €50,000 without a bank account. And on Planet Bertie, climate change doesn't exist." Gormley also could not resist a rather catty little dig at Michael McDowell of the Progressive Democrats (PDs), his Dublin South-East constituency rival and then Tánaiste, whom he described as the "Tammy Wynette of Irish politics, standing desperately by his man Bertie."

What had prompted these insults, just some 80 days out from a general election and so dangerously close to the date on which the Greens would go into coalition with both Fianna Fáil and the remnants of the PDs?

There had been the explosive disclosure by *The Irish Times* in September 2006 that the Mahon tribunal was investigating payments of between €50,000 and €100,000 from business people for Ahern's personal use when he was minister for finance in 1993. Ahern maintained the money being investigated had been provided by friends as a "dig out" following his marriage separation. The tribunal of inquiry into planning matters and payments, which would eventually bring about Ahern's premature exit from frontline politics, was in fact established by his first government in 1997. Initially operating under the chairmanship of Mr Justice Fergus Flood, it was originally known as the Flood Tribunal and continued its work under Judge Alan Mahon.

Prior to the 2007 election, the Greens had pointedly refused to rule out coalition with Fianna Fáil, although Trevor Sargent, then still at the helm of the party, said he would resign rather than lead his colleagues into such an administration. Sargent did not believe the Greens were handicapped in the post-election Government-forming negotiations as a consequence of Gormley having ventilated his true thoughts on the inhabitants of "Planet Bertie", however. "No, it was better that Fianna Fáil knew where they stood with us and we knew where we stood with them. I don't want to call it a marriage of convenience because that would be an abuse of the term marriage, but it was a working arrangement," Sargent said.

He was true to his word about not leading the party into power with Fianna Fáil, although he did accept a junior ministerial position. This was a contortion that left Ahern bemused. Ahern's view was that Sargent had "tied himself in knots" by resigning the leadership, refusing a seat in Cabinet and then taking a junior minister's post, that of Minister of State at the Department of Agriculture, Food and Fisheries, with special responsibility for Food and Horticulture. "I'm sure there was a point of principle in there somewhere, although it was lost on me," he later scoffed in his autobiography published in 2009 entitled *Bertie*.

Sargent subsequently shrugged off the criticism when relating what happened at a meeting between Ahern and himself after the Programme for Government deal was nailed down and they were determining which person from which party should get what job. "I don't expect Bertie to understand where the Greens are coming from. He said to me, 'You'll take a senior ministry' and I said, 'I can't,' I said, 'I can't because I've given an undertaking.' He said, 'Ah don't worry about that.'" Sargent recalled. He said Ahern was laughing as he suggested people would forget all about the pre-election promise. But Ahern was not the only one to be scornful of Sargent's moral manoeuvrings. His colleague Paul Gogarty claimed to have told Sargent well before the election that his stance simply did not make sense. Gogarty, who insisted there was "no damn difference" between Fianna Fáil and Fine Gael, later complained about the "stupidity" of what he described as Sargent's "morally tangled" decision of not leading the party into Government with Fianna Fáil but then accepting a junior ministry. Sargent's argument was that he and many others in the party, among whom he included Gormley, desired "total change" at Government level – in other words, the departure of Fianna Fáil from power – "but it was not a position party members were prepared to take publicly because [they] did not want to do anything that would hamstring them from having policies implemented."

Disapproving of what he considered such a "promiscuous" stance on coalition options, a matter he was regularly quizzed about by journalists and constituents, Sargent said he resolved to take a personal stand. "The party was always going to be creating the impression that it was completely promiscuous as to what its options were and I felt there was a need to provide some level of stability to that question, and I suppose effectively put myself in the position of being a potential sacrificial lamb," he said. In Sargent's mind, there was no sense of moral confusion at all about the position he took. "It's very black and white really; there's no great mystery about it," he said. The way he thought about it, the party could eventually decide to do whatever the party decided to do, but he told colleagues: "I will not lead the party into government with Fianna Fáil because I really do believe they've been in government too long and the culture of close association between vested interests and politics has to be broken."

To this day, the Greens cannot agree among themselves as to

why Ahern asked them to join his third Government. Some put the political experiment down to a quirk in Ahern's personality, or a desire to put a trendy tinge on the faded colour scheme of his administration, as the Greens were neither necessary for a majority nor figuring in the governing option he preferred initially, while others insisted the move was simply an insurance policy to ensure the Coalition's longevity. Initially, Ahern made it known that he would favour a deal with the remnants of the PDs and like-minded Independents who had emerged from the so-called Fianna Fáil 'gene pool'. Such an arrangement would have granted Ahern a majority in the Dáil, similar to his 1997 achievement, and negotiations aimed at facilitating such an arrangement got underway in the days immediately after the election. He then made the surprise move of offering to negotiate with the Greens as well.

Gormley felt a timely approach to the Greens allowed Ahern to give a Fianna Fáil-led Government a dimension it would have previously lacked. Ahern had observed the issue of global warming and other environmental matters dominating the international news agenda and finally making inroads into the domestic media prior to the election, and sensed the Greens could add something new to his administration. However, the inclusive move, although bold, could not be viewed as entirely altruistic, Gormley conceded. "No, Bertie was fairly genuine on this issue. But of course it also meant that he did not have to hand out as many Ministries to Labour if that had been the coalition."

Dan Boyle believed formulating the third Ahern-led

Government was simply a numbers game for the then taoiseach, with the Greens brought in only to bolster the majority. "That was an insurance policy. They would have become a minority party government quite quickly. It was quite clear he was going to have further trouble with the tribunal; that the PDs would have gone out of existence quite quickly. And the Independent members, there weren't enough of them and they could not be relied on," Boyle figured. He reckoned very few senior members of Fianna Fáil, including Ahern and Cowen, ever really understood where the Greens were coming from with their environmental agenda. Donall Geoghegan, the Green's general secretary who would be appointed programme manager once a deal was struck, also doubted ideology ever came into the equation at all. "He's not that kind of fellow ... ideology and Bertie don't go together. No, I don't think so for a minute. It's pure politics, pure and utter. Get the job done, and it's not even an attempt to own the Green vote ... No, pure politics," Geoghegan insisted. Sargent said bringing the Greens into power meant there was "one less Opposition element" for Ahern to deal with. "He'd been slagging me off about swans and snails and all the rest of it, and me accusing him of a few things as well, so I guess he wanted a bit of a break from all that," Sargent said.

Whatever his reasoning, once Ahern extended his hand to the Greens, the Fianna Fáil negotiating team set about meeting the smaller party's reference group to see if their respective pre-election promises could be accommodated into a Programme for Government. Political heavyweights Brian Cowen, Noel Dempsey and the late Seamus Brennan lined up for the Fianna Fáil team. The Greens' negotiators comprised Gormley, Boyle and Geoghegan, with the chairwoman of the party's national council Trish Forde-Brennan and national co-ordinator Councillor Dominick Donnelly also involved. Cowen, Ahern's pugilistic second-in-command who would go on to replace him as leader of Fianna Fáil and Taoiseach, was bullish throughout and certainly never betrayed any feelings of warmth towards the Greens for as long as the negotiations lasted. Referring to the PDs many years previously, Cowen brusquely told delegates at the 1992 Fianna Fáil Ard Fheis: "When in doubt, leave them out." The Greens negotiators were left in no doubt that Cowen harboured a similarly hostile attitude to power-sharing with their party.

Dempsey was a policy wonk and happy to get stuck into a detailed debate with his prospective coalition partners. He was genuinely interested in teasing out the nitty-gritty of what some of the Greens' more interesting theories, so far untested, might mean in reality. Sargent said the Greens were lucky Dempsey was involved, because he was one of the few Fianna Fáil figures who seemed prepared to go public with concerns about the environment. "He appreciated that we had to make a transition to a fossil fuel free future, so we were fortunate in that sense," Sargent said.

But all agreed that the approachable Brennan provided the glue that would ultimately bind the two very different parties together. It was Brennan who greeted the Greens with the immortal line which, while friendly, served to remind the junior partners of their relative inexperience: "You are playing senior hurling now lads, but you are playing with lads with All-Ireland medals." Geoghegan remembered Brennan, who died in July 2008, behaved in quite a kindly manner to the Greens throughout the negotiations and beyond. "Seamus Brennan was very helpful and very approachable. Obviously as he got ill he wasn't around as much, but I remember him vividly through the negotiations of the first programme and how he worked people, was able to work his own side quite well, get them together and get them working as well as they could," Geoghegan recalled. "Seamus Brennan kind of held it together to a great extent."

The Greens knew they did not have a strong hand going into the negotiations. Not only had they no experience of such high-level talks with seasoned professionals, but they were still reeling from an unexpectedly poor showing in the recent general election. Prior to the 2007 poll, backroom staff had been busily preparing for power and the Greens had deemed themselves ready to step up from the Opposition ditch and play what Brennan termed "senior hurling." It would be forgotten soon after they got their feet under the Cabinet table, but the May election result was very disappointing for the Greens and it left them with even less clout than they had been expecting to wield in discussions to form a coalition.

Commentators on the 2007 election constantly spoke of smaller parties being 'squeezed' by the big two, being Fianna Fáil and Fine Gael of course. This image of tiny ants being trampled by fighting elephants was an interpretation the Green leadership was happy to concur with by way of an explanation for the failure of the party's campaign strategy. But this was by no means the only factor. Grumbling political opponents claimed that a growing awareness of environmental issues, combined with gloom-laden pronouncements about global warming, meant the nightly television news could often appear like a broadcast on behalf of the Greens, but the party somehow failed to capitalise on their new-found relevance. Astonishingly, the Greens only just managed to scrape back to the 30th Dáil with the same number of seats they held in the 29th, after gaining one TD and losing another. The actual vote garnered by the party, at 4.7 per cent, was considerably lower than the six to eight per cent the opinion polls had been predicting. The party's expressed target had been to gain in the region of four new seats, as well as holding existing posts, which would have pushed its Dáil representation into double figures for the first time.

Mary White, a "newcomer" after two unsuccessful general election attempts, managed to make the grade in Carlow-Kilkenny, but Boyle, who had represented Cork South-Central for five years, lost his position. Returned again were Sargent on the eighth of ten counts in Dublin North; Eamon Ryan on the eighth and penultimate count in Dublin South and Gogarty on the sixth and final count in Dublin Mid-West. Gormley eventually saw off his arch enemy McDowell to take the last seat in Dublin South-East, although there were only 304 votes in it when transfers were distributed, and Ciaran Cuffe came close to losing his seat after initially polling far behind Richard Boyd-Barrett of People Before Profit in Dún Laoghaire.

The Green parliamentarians, elected under the complex Irish system of proportional representation by means of a single transferable vote in multi-seat constituencies (PR-STV), had a keen sense of being part of an international movement. They kept in close contact with Greens who had tasted power elsewhere and they knew the experience of government had proved extremely bruising for their colleagues in other countries. And even within Ireland, the Greens had a clear and recent example from the previous administration of what type of fate could befall a junior partner to Fianna Fáil. The small PDs, so reviled by the Greens that Gormley and McDowell had an unedifying open air public spat in the middle of the Dublin South-East constituency that became known as the "Rumble in Ranelagh", had just been chewed up and spat out by the electorate.

The aforementioned duel took place after the then PD leader attempted to reprise his successful pre-election stunt of 2002 when, in a well-timed intervention, he used a ladder to climb a lamppost and erect a poster warning about the possibility of a return to single-party Fianna Fáil government. Returning to the same spot during the 2007 campaign, McDowell unveiled a similar poster railing against the formation of a "left-wing" government involving Labour. A furious Gormley arrived on the scene to hijack the PD media event, clutching a leaflet McDowell's workers had distributed which he claimed distorted Green policies. The bespectacled rivals went toe to toe in a confrontation captured for posterity by chuckling reporters, photographers, TV cameramen and other curious onlookers. The unseemly row did neither man any favours, although the Greens had grown so desperate they were pathetically grateful for the media attention. Geoghegan recalled Green candidates and backroom workers had been in despair during the election campaign because they felt they were failing to secure remotely adequate press coverage. "And then fair play to John Gormley for doing his thing in Ranelagh, which was great from our perspective. It got us on the map again. It was enough to give us some presence at least," Geoghegan said.

"We struggled through that campaign, we were lucky to hold onto six seats," he admitted. "I mean Ciaran Cuffe nearly lost his seat. Dan lost his. Mary picked up hers, fair play to her, against the odds you could say through just very hard campaigning on the ground on her part ... Going back with six seats was good in the circumstances."

So the Green leadership can hardly be blamed for wanting to seize the chance to enter Government after the 2007 election. They reckoned this would be their best, perhaps their only, chance to taste political office for quite some time. But it meant that the problems exposed by the 2007 election, most seriously what Boyle described as the party's "shrinking" vote in constituencies, were not resolved. The more perceptive among the Greens must have known that an association with Fianna Fáil policies would go on to destroy what was perhaps their greatest asset, their previous "transfer-friendly" status, which had seen them attract votes — albeit not first preferences — from people traditionally loyal to more established parties across the political divide.

Late one evening in May shortly after the votes were counted, as a Sunday night turned into a Monday morning, Cuffe went online and fired off a number of remarks highly critical of Fianna Fáil and Ahern. He published the cutting comments on his Cuffe Street blog at 12.35 am on May 28th. "Ouch. That was close," he began, in reference to the extremely narrow retention of his seat. "Let's be clear. A deal with Fianna Fáil would be a deal with the devil. We would be spat out after five years, and decimated as a party. But ... would it be worth it? Power is a many-faceted thing," he wrote.

Cuffe expressed a worry about what he described as Ahern's "moral compass" and said Fianna Fáil could not be changed, "if their only measure of success is cranes on the skyline." He remains unrepentant about his late-night musings today.

"I thought Fianna Fáil would be wiped out in '97. Didn't happen. I thought the same thing in 2002. Didn't happen. So 2007, if you can't beat them work with them. Not join them, but work with them to try and get policy enacted," he said.

"I'd been waiting around for a quarter of a century in a party. When you're in a small party and an opportunity comes along you take it. You could be the hurler on the ditch all your life and some NGOs are, some commentators are and some politicians are."

According to Gormley, it was not until the Greens were actually in the process of negotiating the Programme for Government that they were made aware by Brennan that Mary Harney was "in the shake-up" as well, and was in fact also inside Government Buildings on Merrion Street. Amazingly, despite a disastrous performance in the election, the PDs somehow managed to emerge as pivotal to the formation of the new Government. The junior partner in the second Ahern-led Government had entered the 2007 election with eight TDs and emerged with just two: Harney and Noel Grealish. After McDowell's defeat, Harney had temporarily resumed the leadership of the PDs, an honour that would soon pass to Ciaran Cannon, a Senator who would rise to become a Fine Gael junior minister in 2011. Grealish's continued focus on local issues in his Galway West constituency, allied with his refusal to waste energy building a national profile through media interventions, saved his seat while his colleagues sank without trace. Those who lost their positions along with McDowell were the party's chief whip Liz O'Donnell; ministers of state Tom Parlon and Tim O'Malley, and backbenchers Fiona O'Malley and Mae Sexton. Sexton would go on to unsuccessfully contest the 2011 general election for the Labour Party.

The news that Ahern wished to retain the services of Harney was not welcomed by the Greens. "That was a problem because we were never enthusiastic about the PDs," Gormley said, with some degree of understatement. He largely blamed PD policy for the excesses of the boom years. "When you do the analysis, the real difficulty occurred between 2002 and 2007. That's when you had all these crazy things happening: increases in expenditure and cutting of taxes. It's just a recipe for disaster ... we didn't readily identify at all with a lot of the PD stuff." However, Gormley would go on to develop a "good, fine personal relationship" with Harney.

"I found her to be a nice person and very helpful indeed actually," he said. Geoghegan believed the change of leadership at the top of the PDs had helped sweeten the pill for Gormley, and the Greens found it particularly easy to deal with Harney's gentlemanly special adviser on health policy Oliver O'Connor. "Because we had a quite anti-PD thing going on when John took on McDowell out in Ranelagh and all that, if McDowell had still been there I don't think it would have been do-able," Geoghegan said. Ryan also established a good relationship with Harney, Geoghegan added, and a decent working arrangement soon developed between the two small parties with such diverse agendas. "The PDs sent out a signal very early on in our term of Government to us that they wanted to accommodate, they wanted to be helpful," Geoghegan confirmed. Boyle said the Green's preference "from day one" would have been for Harney not to be involved again in Cabinet, although he did concede that she was "supportive of John" during subsequent discussions.

In contrast to both the Greens and the PDs, Fianna Fáil had had a surprisingly good election, despite a troubled campaign dominated by Ahern's personal finances. There were many awkward moments for Ahern and the party in the run-up to the only poll that mattered, but Fianna Fáil's fate was somehow salvaged by the brute force and legendary organisational capabilities of Cowen. While Fianna Fáil returned with a slightly reduced number of seats, 78 compared to 81, the party's vote was actually up a little from its healthy 2002 result. The first round of talks with Fianna Fáil ended in deadlock, but any roadblocks were worked through. As environmental issues had finally become fashionable in Ireland, the skilfully-crafted Fianna Fáil manifesto had contained a series of commitments on such matters and Green negotiators got very little policy accepted beyond those. The Greens also grudgingly agreed to the continuation of the contentious and now defunct PD policy on hospital co-location, involving the building of private hospitals on the grounds of public facilities, which was that party's bottom line in the talks. "Yeah, that was difficult," Geoghegan recalled.

However, while the Green negotiators knew they had been out-witted to some extent, they finally felt in a position to present a draft version of the Programme for Government to the party membership at what would turn out to be an emotional meeting held in the Mansion House in Dublin on 13 June. Cuffe would utilise his blog again on the day the Green grassroots were asked to rubber-stamp the Programme for Government. Writing ahead of the vote and paraphrasing the soccer commentator Eamon Dunphy, Cuffe commented: "It's a good deal, not a great deal." Of the relationship with Fianna Fáil, he predicted it "wouldn't be a marriage made in heaven, but few are these days. And besides, sometimes opposites attract, and maybe a marriage of pragmatism and idealism could last the test of time." In a wry conclusion, he signed off with his view that "sometimes the devil has all the best tunes."

Prominent among the Green dissenters at the Mansion House was the former MEP for Dublin Patricia McKenna, who complained about the party's failure to end the use of Shannon Airport by US troops en route to Iraq. Criticism was also prompted by the party's inability to alter Government policy on the controversial M3 motorway route, which planned to cut a swathe through the Hill of Tara. There were other compromises, with a number of treasured policies effectively abandoned, but the leadership persuaded the grassroots the price was worth paying. Boyle was among the senior members who shed tears when party members voted by an overwhelming 86 per cent to enter government. A total of 510 votes were cast, with members voting 441 to 67 in favour of the leadership's proposal. Two of those eligible spoiled their votes. Speaking after the result was announced, Sargent told members the day was the proudest of his life. He also took the opportunity to formally announce he would keep his commitment to stand down as leader, but would remain as acting leader until a successor was chosen by complete mandate of all members.

With the programme for government nailed down, Sargent and Ahern met in the taoiseach's office to discuss the allocation of jobs. The two men agreed the position of Minister for the

Environment, a post previously held by Dick Roche of Fianna Fáil, would go to Gormley. But Sargent was unable to wrestle the Department of Transport from Fianna Fáil's grasp. "I went in there very keen that Eamon Ryan would become the Minister for Transport," Sargent said. "But I think Bertie had set his face against that one." The Greens wanted Transport, Sargent explained, "because of the transformation that was needed in the shift from road to public transport spending; the rail-lines that needed to be re-opened; Metro North; electrification; the national cycling strategy." It was most unlikely Fianna Fáil would ever relinquish transport – in those days a high-spending department – to the cycling Greens. As it happened, Sargent was not unhappy with Ahern's choice of Dempsey for Minister for Transport. "We were fortunate that we had somebody like Noel Dempsey in the Department of Transport because Noel, to use the parlance, 'got it.'"

Anyway, Sargent did well to secure the title of Minister for Energy, Communications and Natural Resources – Dempsey's old post, as it happened – for Ryan. "Eamon was very happy with Energy, Communications and Natural Resources, and I think in many ways that was a very critical infrastructural and strategic portfolio for us to have," Sargent said. Ryan concurred enthusiastically: "I was in about the best ministry I could ever be in. I mean, I just loved it really. I'd spent ten years preparing for it: our five years in opposition and then prior to that. I knew more about it than any other politician. Now that sounds immodest, I knew about it because I was on the Oireachtas committee [for Communications, Marine and Natural Resources] for five years and that gives you a training, and so I loved it."

So while they tried and failed to get their hands on the transport portfolio, the Greens did manage to secure two powerful Cabinet positions, along with one junior ministry with the promise of another minister of state's position half way through the Government's term. And so the Greens began tentatively feeling their way along the corridors of power. They shed their Opposition image as a bunch of professional refuseniks to vote for Ahern as taoiseach in a Government backed by 90 TDs, including four of the five Independents. Jackie Healy-Rae, Finian McGrath, Michael Lowry and Beverley Flynn all struck deals with Ahern; Tony Gregory, who died in January 2009, was the only Independent who managed to resist his charms.

CHAPTER 3

MEET THE NEW BOSSES

IT SEEMED A FOREGONE CONCLUSION THAT JOHN GORMLEY, WHO had spent ten years in the Dáil and was now a cabinet minister, would replace acting leader Trevor Sargent at the top of the party in July 2007. The dissident Patricia McKenna, who had opposed going into Government with Fianna Fáil, mounted a stronger than expected challenge, however.

While Sargent denied Gormley was his anointed or obvious successor, as Fianna Fáil leader Bertie Ahern had so recently described Finance Minister Brian Cowen, he understood that the practicalities of day-to-day politics meant the new leader simply had to be drawn from the ranks of elected members.

"I felt it needed to be someone in the parliamentary party for Government to work. That didn't stop Patricia McKenna from thinking otherwise," Sargent recalled. Nevertheless, Gormley was elected leader by an almost two-thirds majority, with 478 votes or 65% of the ballot, compared to the 263 votes or 35% secured by McKenna. The McKenna challenge, although ultimately unsuccessful, was something of an early warning signal for the party leadership, representing a desire among Green activists for the party to retain its independence within Government. Their message was that any hint that the lines between the new Coalition partners were being allowed to blur would be punished severely.

Sargent admitted the role he performed as leader was completely different from the position Gormley shouldered. Leading a small, generally well-liked party in Opposition, Sargent had the luxury of time which he used to travel around the country, from Letterkenny in Co. Donegal to Clonakilty in Co. Cork, keeping in touch with the grassroots. "Whereas in the case of John he was locked into a high profile Coalition Government role and so the scope that he had for doing any of that travelling ... was quite confined." Gormley, on the other hand, was at the head of the party that had put Fianna Fáil back into power, in the view of many external observers. Gormley was not unaware of the danger of drifting out of contact with the party faithful while attending to Cabinet duties, however, and let it be known that he was determined that the responsibilities attached to his post as Minister for the Environment would not distract him from his other new job as leader of the Greens. The beginning of the party's time in high office was hardly a honeymoon, but the Greens surprised many observers of politics with their unexpected lack of flakiness and unity of purpose in the early days. There were some teething problems, to be sure. When Gormley attended his first pre-Cabinet breakfast, he found the atmosphere strange and subdued. Deeming his fellow Ministers a decidedly unfriendly bunch, Gormley munched his muesli in silence as they polished off their sausages and bacon. It was not until he got up to leave the room that one member of Cabinet took pity on him and said, "You do know that this is the Fianna Fáil pre-Cabinet breakfast?" Gormley and Ryan made do with chopped-up fruit in a small sideroom in future.

The Greens undoubtedly brought a certain level of novelty to the administration which, as Ahern had no doubt anticipated, reflected favourably on his new Government. Cycling remained the Green Ministers' favourite mode of transport, whatever the weather, despite the presence of Garda drivers who came with the job. Gormley pedalled from his home in Ringsend to Government Buildings on Merrion Street and back whenever he could. His Ministerial car was an environmentally-friendly Toyota Prius, which reduced the guilt factor when he was obliged to travel on four wheels. Ryan also tried to stick to the Greens' 'two wheels good, four wheels bad' philosophy. He was comfortable in the saddle, having previously headed the Dublin Cycling Campaign and pushed for bike lanes in the capital. Before the political bug bit, he had run a cycling safaris business. Gormley and Ryan were obviously not typical Irish Ministers and, with agendas and attitudes strikingly different from that of their Fianna Fáil counterparts, they began attempting to put a distinctive Green stamp on their individual departments. Officials in Gormley's office, the graceful Custom House building overlooking the River Liffey, exchanged alarmed glances when he asked if they had a presence on something called "the blogosphere" at an early meeting. Ryan's Secretary General presented him with a box set of *Yes Minister* DVDs as a humorous welcoming gift to his Department in Adelaide Road.

As programme manager Donall Geoghegan recalled, the arrival of the Green Ministers was a shock to the system for some of the civil servants. "We had more of an agenda in Environment and Energy than previous ministers and we were different," he said. Gormley, who had pledged to put climate change at the top of his programme of reform, was succeeding Fianna Fáil's Dick Roche, "so there was quite a reorientation there." Ryan had been preceded by the Fianna Fáil Minister Noel Dempsey, who, as has been noted, was somewhat more in tune with Green thinking. "During the first year there was a lot of concentration on the two lads doing their thing in their Departments, and Trevor as well in Agriculture. So there was a lot of groundwork done during that time," Geoghegan said. The appointment of two Green Senators by Taoiseach Bertie Ahern in August 2007 bulked the party's parliamentary representation up to eight. Dan Boyle was made deputy leader of the new Seanad and Deirdre de Burca, who had unsuccessfully contested the Dáil election for a second time in Wicklow, was also among the Taoiseach's nominees. De Burca had a background as a primary school teacher and psychologist, and was then viewed as having good long-term prospects in the party.

The party leadership also managed to convince a few poachers to turn gamekeepers, which proved crucial to amplifying any initial successes they achieved. Among those who came to work for the

Greens on the communications front was the experienced journalist John Downing, who became deputy Government press secretary and spokesman for the Greens in Government. The straight-talking Downing was previously political correspondent of the *Irish Daily Star* and held senior positions in a number of national broadsheet newspapers. Never in any danger of going native with the Greens, he brought an awareness of life on both sides of the political fence to his often frank interactions with former colleagues in the Dáil press corps. The ultra-conscientious Liam Reid left his position as environment correspondent with *The Irish Times* after being recruited by Gormley as an adviser with a media relations and policy role at the Department of the Environment. Evidently a natural environmentalist, Reid and his family once spent a week trying to live without producing any non-recyclable rubbish for a newspaper assignment. Other smart hires included the intelligent Brid McGrath, Ryan's Departmental spokeswoman and press adviser, whose breezy, quirky nature was a perfect match for the Green's slightly alternative way of working, while the always calm former party official Ryan Meade was promoted to the position of policy adviser to Gormley. Heading up the party's press office was a likeable and hard-working Northerner, Damian Connon, valued by the Greens as a technical whizz-kid. Connon was assisted by Nicola Cassidy, a very able press officer by day and a glamorous singer with the popular band Electric Avenue by night.

Quiet progress was made on the policy front at this time, with the Green Ministers unveiling draft building regulations applying to new planning applications aimed at improving energy efficiency and reducing CO2 emissions. In another new departure, the Government said it would buy carbon offsets to cover the carbon dioxide emissions created by a business trip Ryan was taking to the United States. However, there would be further trouble in north Mayo, where the Corrib gas dispute continued, although at this early stage Shell to Sea campaigners welcomed Ryan's appointment, saying it offered an opportunity to resolve the situation. Meanwhile, the contract for the controversial Ringsend incinerator was signed, shortly after Gormley had reiterated his opposition to the project of that type in his constituency.

RELATIONS WITH FIANNA FÁIL WERE MORE THAN CORDIAL TO BEGIN but one issue that had been bubbling under the surface soon came to dominate political discourse and would put the Greens through the horrors. The Mahon tribunal resumed its deliberations in Dublin Castle, the former seat of British rule in Ireland, shortly after the election and Ahern started to give his long-awaited evidence concerning his personal finances in September 2007. The Taoiseach, who was convinced the tribunal was partial, reasserted that he had never accepted money for improper purposes and said he had not kept accounts of his earnings and expenditure. As the days passed, however, he began to face boos and catcalls from members of the public outside Dublin Castle. Ahern's increasingly disastrous appearances before the tribunal were a huge distraction to the business of governing, Geoghegan recalled. "There was a lot of discomfort, quite deep discomfort, with what was going on there and there were some difficult dealings with Fianna Fáil in Government at that time." The Greens were in an increasingly tricky position. Having been such vocal critics of Ahern's personal finances before the election, sometimes going where other parties had feared to tread, now in Government they could only repeat the mantra that the tribunal must be allowed to complete its business. They risked getting into an even stickier situation when Fine Gael, probably rueing its pre-election timidity on the subject, put down a motion of no confidence in Ahern on the day the Dáil resumed after its summer break.

The drafting of the counter-motion did not go smoothly, Geoghegan remembered, given the tense atmosphere in what had by then become Ahern's bunker in Government Buildings. The Greens were unhappy because the motion drafted by the Fianna Fáil side of the house did not initially display explicit support for the Mahon tribunal. "I can remember meetings with quite a bit of tension as we, for example, were putting together agreed lines for the motions ... we insisted for example in confidence in the Mahon tribunal, something that was complete anathema for the lads upstairs," he said.

"A massive bunker was being built, it was growing and growing, that siege mentality that became the last year of Bertie Ahern as Taoiseach." All TDs from the Government benches were summoned to the chamber for the late night vote, which the coalition won by 81 votes to 76. The Greens were left feeling badly bruised by the episode, however, having been roundly mocked by the Opposition parties. Fine Gael leader Enda Kenny threw their campaigning words back in their faces with some relish. "We remember the slogan 'Green politics is clean politics.' Now, Green politics is blind politics as Deputies Gormley, Ryan and Sargent adopt the standards we have come to associate with the Progressive Democrats," Kenny cried. He then zoned in on the man widely viewed as the conscience of the Green Party: "Last year Deputy Sargent, a man of impeccable standards and principles, sat on this side of the House as an admirable man who week after week rose to his feet to excoriate Fianna Fáil and the Taoiseach, in particular, for the lack of standards manifest in his taking of money. He now sits behind the Taoiseach, his mind utterly changed having been seduced by the attraction of power." Eamon Gilmore, who had just taken over the leadership of the Labour Party from Pat Rabbitte, claimed the Greens had "turned yellow." He added: "It cannot but be a source of deep regret to those of us who support progressive politics and standards in public life that the Green Party should have sold out so comprehensively and so quickly."

And there was worse to come from the tribunal. The Taoiseach and his colleagues were increasingly rattled by the hearings at Dublin Castle, leaving observers both inside and outside Government wondering how long Ahern could feasibly continue at the helm without utterly destabilising the three-party administration. Ryan found himself increasingly exasperated, believing that the tribunal situation was becoming "impossible". He was keen that the Greens avoid making the same mistake as the PDs in the previous administration when the junior partner got wobbly about Ahern's evidence during the election campaign and threatened to pull out of government, only to decide to remain in power. Gormley too knew the drip-drip of tribunal stories dominating media coverage at the time was impeding his party's progress in Government. "Everything we were trying to do was completely undermined in a sense by this elephant in the room," Gormley said. The Green strategy was to maintain that the party had to avoid at all costs taking on the role of watchdog in Government, or else run the risk of being able to devote no time at all to implementing policy. As Ciaran Cuffe explained: "Look, let there be no doubt about it, it was an incredibly stressful time when Bertie Ahern was at the tribunal but ... the Greens were not and could not be the moral guardians of Fianna Fáil. We were in there to deliver a programme and if we spent our time examining the perceived moral failings of Fianna Fáil that could take up every moment of our time. That was my strong view."

More revelations followed. The most serious was that a house had been bought by Ahern's former partner Celia Larkin in 1993 with money that had been donated to his constituency organisation in Drumcondra. The loan was paid back after the tribunal began to make enquiries about the issue. Then there was dramatic evidence from a mother of three youngsters Gráinne Carruth, Ahern's former secretary, who broke down in tears in the witness box as she accepted she had lodged sterling to Ahern's account, despite previous evidence. "I just want to go home," the weeping witness said. After that, Ahern had lost the confidence of the Fianna Fáil organisation. The Greens needed to say something, and fast. Councillor Niall Ó Brolcháin, a former lord mayor of Galway, stepped forward and called on Ahern to resign. He pointed out the Greens' national conference in Dundalk, Co. Louth, was looming, and certain to be dominated by the topic. Boyle was also horrified, and said so. Fiona O'Malley, a PD senator, called for clarification from the Taoiseach, saying the Government's credibility was being undermined by the tribunal disclosures about his finances. Her party colleague Mary Harney began to talk about "public disquiet", piling further pressure on the Green leadership to speak out.

Finally – and not before time – the Green leadership cracked, with Gormley too calling on Ahern to make a clarifying statement, citing growing public concern as his motivation. "There is evidence of growing public interest in this issue and there are concerns. More information from the Taoiseach would help here," he said at the time. "I think the Taoiseach is a very experienced politician. I think he knows it's in his best interest and that of his party and the country at large that a clarifying statement is made." Looking back with hindsight, Gormley said: "It was total distraction and eventually that's why he decided to go, because it was a distraction." Eventually indeed.

Although it would be May 2008 before Ahern finally tendered his resignation as prime minister, he made the shock announcement on 2 April that he would step down. Aged 56, he had served as the so-called 'Teflon Taoiseach' for 11 years, the man to whom nothing could stick. The country's second longest-serving Taoiseach, he came second only to Eamon de Valera, the founder of Fianna Fáil.

The great majority of his Cabinet colleagues had only fully understood his intentions when he told them at a meeting early that morning. They were gob-smacked. There were tears from some of the women, and quite a number of the men including Ahern himself. Even the bruiser Cowen's emotions got the better of him. A disconsolate Ahern told his colleagues he was heading for the ceremonial staircase to face the huge crowd of reporters, photographers and television camera crew members jammed inside the door of Government Buildings at short notice. With a sigh, he told the bewildered Ministers to join him if they wanted, although they did not have to.

Eyebrows were raised when Gormley was one of those who appeared behind Ahern as he emerged from the shadows and approached the lectern to make his resignation speech in front of the richly-coloured stained-glass window, flanked by grim-faced senior Fianna Fáil colleagues. Most of them filtered down the steps to stand in front of Ahern or on the same level. Cowen remained at Ahern's left hand and Dempsey at his right, with Brian Lenihan and others behind. Gormley's presence was immortalised in still photographs and televised footage of the day, with his image framed in every shot. He blamed it on his height, which meant he towered over smaller figures like Martin Cullen. "It's funny, I was actually standing at the back but because many of the Cabinet were small in stature I was one of the few visible in the shot," he said. Although he faced criticism, Gormley maintains he made the right decision.

"I went down because it was the decent and right thing to do. He had asked members of the Cabinet to go down with him, if they wanted. I was a member of his Cabinet; he had appointed me as a Minister. It was right to stand with him on his last day," he said. "I didn't even think about it I just said, 'This is the decent thing to do'. I don't believe at all in kicking people when they're down." Ryan obviously did not think it was a good judgement call by Gormley to have joined Ahern, but then he had not attended the meeting and so did not have to make the decision which would come back to haunt the Green leader.

Ahern was finally gone, although he embarked on a carefully choreographed lap of honour, with numerous high-profile engagements at which he cited peace in Northern Ireland as his proudest achievement. Even at that stage, observers tentatively wondered if his future might include a tilt at the Presidency, or perhaps a high-profile post in Europe, but it was not to be. Brennan discreetly resigned on the same day for health reasons.

Cowen, the long-time Fianna Fáil leader-in-waiting, then 48 years old, took Ahern's place as expected after being elected leader at a parliamentary party meeting. He was subsequently elected Taoiseach in the Dáil, by 88 votes to 76. He had served a long political apprenticeship, having been first elected to the Dáil in 1984 at the age of 24, when he won the Laois-Offaly by-election brought about by the death of his father Bernard. Boyle said the Greens, along with others in political circles, were far from surprised by the appointment. "We went into Government in the full expectation that Bertie was going to be leaving eventually anyway and also in the expectation that Cowen more than likely was going to be taking over from him. So that was known," Boyle said. "He did seem to have a bit of a wind behind him," he conceded. That was putting it mildly. Fianna Fáil got a significant boost in popular support in opinion polls as a result of the perceived fresh start.

The Greens looked on as Cowen, excited and daunted in equal measure, embarked on a homecoming tour to his native county of Offaly. The town of Clara never look as well as it prepared for the return of its most successful son, and provided a rapturous reception when the new Taoiseach turned up in triumph. Pints of beer were drunk and champagne guzzled as the photographers snapped happily, and Cowen delivered passionate speeches at open-air rallies and sang heartily at pit-stops throughout his constituency, including Tullamore where he lived. There was no sense of trepidation among the Greens at that early stage in Cowen's leadership: quite the opposite, in fact. Looking back at the transition period when the centre of power shifted from Ahern to Cowen, Geoghegan could recall only a sense of relief. "When we were dealing with Bertie, that took up a lot more of my time than I would have wished. But look, we negotiated our way through it, we were able to deal with it, I thought quite well, and to an extent the prospect of Cowen coming in felt like a little bit of a relief," Geoghegan said.

"We knew Cowen. We knew what he was like, we knew his bully-boy tactics and that kind of stuff but still: he's human, he's a nice fellow," Geoghegan said.

Ryan concurred, to a degree, recalling that the opinion poll ratings for Cowen had "gone through the roof" at that time. "It was widely welcomed. To be honest I was personally relieved that there was a change because I think the whole Mahon Tribunal hearings were just becoming impossible. And there was a certain sense of relief that at least wasn't going to dominate and was not going to continue in terms of being at the very centre of Government and political discourse," he said. "I don't have a sense that we were there elated in terms of, 'Oh great, here's Brian Cowen, yippee!' It was just a matter of just going to sit down and work with whoever it is."

The reliable Cowen would steady the ship of State and would certainly not produce any controversy, the Greens thought, and they looked forward to settling down to a quiet, policy-focused life in Government. With Ahern finally on the brink of being consigned to the backbenches, and the distraction of the Mahon tribunal behind them, the Greens set about trying to get some belated credit for their small but nonetheless not insignificant achievements during their 10-month stint in Government. Appealing almost exclusively to their base, they talked-up the reintroduction of the white-tailed sea eagle to Co. Kerry. Also highlighted were emissions-based motor taxes and an allocation of €26 million for wave power, as well as the ESB's commitment to generate one-third of energy needs from renewable sources by 2020.

THE DRAMATIC WALK-OUT OF THE CHINESE AMBASSADOR, LIU Biwei, at the Green's annual conference in April 2008 over Gormley's remarks on human rights in Tibet bolstered the party leader's popularity amongst the grassroots. Although Gormley pulled his punches ever so slightly by referring merely to "abuse", rather than the "flagrant abuse" his script had tantalisingly promised, the televised departure of the highly-insulted Chinese delegation from the conference proved a talking point and pacified internal critics of the party's performance in Government, temporarily at least. "One country which has been exploited and suppressed and suffered far too long is Tibet. We condemn unequivocally the abuse of human rights by the Chinese government and call on the Chinese government to enter dialogue with the Dalai Lama," Gormley said. The fact that the ensuing diplomatic difficulties made things somewhat uncomfortable for Fianna Fáil did not exactly displease Green activists either.

Meanwhile, the new Taosieach was also scoring some modest personal successes during his brief honeymoon period in office. He reshuffled the Cabinet, installing long-time supporters and fellow scions of political dynasties in key economic ministries by moving Brian Lenihan into finance and making Mary Coughlan Minister for Enterprise, Trade and Employment as well as Tanaiste. Cowen's close friend Batt O'Keeffe became an overnight success having just turned 63 when he was appointed Minister for Education, replacing Mary Hanafin. Among those to retain their old titles were the two Green Ministers, Gormley and Eamon Ryan. Although the May 2008 reshuffle was announced to some acclaim at that time, Dan Boyle was retrospectively critical of Cowen's choices. "He made a very poor Cabinet selection ... the drinking buddies in the Dáil bar and stuff like that. Some of those people just weren't up to the job," Boyle grumbled. Looking back, Boyle claimed to have been almost instantly disheartened by Cowen's performance as Taoiseach. "I suppose the disappointing thing about Brian Cowen was that having taken over that was the time to change things and he was so disinclined to do any change," Boyle said. But Cowen, in the early stages of his time in office, did make some alterations that hinted at the possibility of further reforms to come. There was brief embarrassment when, just 15 days into the job, a Dáil microphone picked up the new Taoiseach's use of an expletive in a conversation with Coughlan when he gruffly urged her to get a handle on price increases, after Labour leader Eamon Gilmore said UK supermarkets' were failing to bring their prices in the State into line with British prices, even though sterling had recently weakened substantially. Cowen instructed Coughlan to start making phonecalls about the issue as soon as possible, and "bring in all those f***ers." This unparliamentary outburst offended the delicate sensibilities of some of the Greens. However, this was quickly forgotten when Cowen took the bold decision to shut down Fianna Fáil's legendary and controversial Galway fundraising tent, where the country's richest property developers, builders and businessmen had hob-nobbed with party politicians for many years at the State's most colourful horseracing meet.

The Greens were growing in confidence, and began to test the waters by making tentative pronouncements outside their three portfolio areas: Environment, Energy and Agriculture. Around this time, there was some disagreement between the Coalition partners over the Civil Partnership Bill, which had been included in the Programme for Government at the insistence of the Greens. Disagreements between the liberal Greens and a conservative rump in Fianna Fáil over the strength of rights for same-sex couples delayed the progress of the complex legislation. Launching a Gay Pride festival in Dublin at the end of May, Gormley acknowledged that the Bill as now envisaged would give only limited rights to gay couples. He explained that as the two largest parties in the Dáil opposed "marriage equality", the Greens believed that legislating for civil partnerships was the best they could do for now by way of recognising and protecting same-sex relationships. It was "a step towards full equality", he said. The Greens also attempted to exert some moral pressure on Fianna Fáil on the nationwide provision of Applied Behavioural Analysis (ABA) for children with autism, while Cuffe submitted proposals on sustainable travel to the Government's transport strategy.

CHAPTER 4

A SHUDDERING END

IT WAS A TIME OF CONSOLIDATING RELATIONSHIPS BETWEEN the various personalities that made up the reshuffled Coalition Government. Ryan and Lenihan, who sat opposite each other at the Cabinet table, became quite close. Ryan, educated at Gonzaga College in Ranelagh, took pleasure in Belvedere College boy Lenihan's lengthy intellectual somersaults at Cabinet meetings, during which he would wave around the pair of spectacles vanity prevented him from wearing in public. "Brian was a very, very capable creative talent, unique, but he was also quixotic," Ryan recalled. Apart from his Adelaide Road headquarters, Ryan had a Ministerial office on Merrion Street, across the so-called "bridge of sighs" that linked Leinster House to Government Buildings. Ryan's room was right at the bottom of the black-and-white chequered corridor, but he took some comfort from having such an esteemed political neighbour. "You had a sense that you're at the absolute tail end of power, except that Brian Lenihan's [office] was right across, was the door opposite. Now he wasn't there a lot of the time because his Finance office was just down the road, but that was always slightly encouraging when someone came to visit you, that you weren't at the complete bowels, the fag end, of the administrative system," Ryan recalled.

Of Lenihan, Ciaran Cuffe recalled that he could at times be at least empathetic to the Green cause, unlike some of his fellow Fianna Fáilers. "I think Lenihan had a decent understanding of us. Some Ministers didn't." Dan Boyle's view was that the relationship with Lenihan was "more positive than negative."

A more unlikely, but self-proclaimed, ally for Ryan was Eamon Ó Cuív, a grandson of Fianna Fáil founder Eamon de Valera, who would become deputy leader of his party after the general election. Brian Cowen had retained Ó Cuív's services at the Department of Community, Rural and Gaeltacht Affairs, sometimes disparagingly nicknamed 'Craggy Island' after the isolated location of the comic character Fr Ted's parochial house. Some of the Greens outside Cabinet did not find the relationship with Ó Cuív so easy, however. "Ó Cuív apparently got on well with John and Eamon but I've always found him difficult," Boyle said. Cuffe recalled ongoing "significant disagreements" with Ó Cuív over sensitive subjects like the National Spatial Strategy. "He espouses rural values; I guess I espouse urban values. That was certainly our difference, the main difference, that I encountered with him," Cuffe said.

Willie O'Dea, who was retained in the Department of Defence, was also a "perceived ally at Cabinet" in the early days at least, according to Boyle, but Dermot Ahern and his new

Department of Justice were viewed as a thorn in the side of the Greens. "Constantly difficult," was Boyle's assessment; "Very businesslike," Cuffe said. Curiously – or perhaps because he knew it would annoy them and their supporters – Ahern was effusive in his praise of the Greens in an in-depth interview in *The Irish Times*. "Ryan was a very bright person ... and Gormley a very good party leader. The Greens compared favourably to the PDs as coalition partners for Fianna Fáil. When the PDs were in Government they used to have a crisis every second week, some of it of their own making. The Greens are not like that. The Greens are much more strategic," said Ahern. Mary Harney would give him a severe ribbing over that one when relationships deteriorated later.

Cuffe put the then Ceann Comhairle John O'Donoghue into a similar category as Ahern. "The likes of Dermot Ahern or John O'Donoghue, there wasn't too much common ground between us on a whole lot of issues." Martin Cullen, the Minister for Arts, Sport and Culture who replaced Seamus Brennan, was described as "a constant irritant at Cabinet" by Boyle, but future Fianna Fáil leader Micheál Martin, then newly-appointed to the Department of Foreign Affairs, enjoyed good relationships with the Greens. Donall Geoghegan recalled: "Martin was fine, you could do business with Micheál. He's a very nice man, easy-going, looking for an angle, looking for a way through things. He's a problem-solver."

The Greens were delighted that Cowen kept Dempsey in the Transport portfolio, but the relationship with Mary Hanafin, demoted to the Department of Social and Family Affairs from Education, was much more difficult. The Greens were later stung when Hanafin's frustration with what she saw as the party's fixation with "hares, stags and badgers" was exposed by the *Irish Independent* from the whistle-blowing organisation Wikileaks, but she had done little to keep her distaste for the junior coalition partner's agenda a secret from the beginning. "I can't say I ever had a particularly close relationship with her," Cuffe admitted. The two were rivals in the over-crowded Dun Laoghaire constituency, of course.

As Ahern's comments illustrated, however, the Greens were learning to be just as pragmatic as Fianna Fáil when it came to maintaining professional relationships. "You develop a working relationship with Fianna Fáil as you do with any political grouping. It's a bit like being in business with somebody: just because you're contractually bound doesn't mean that you agree with that person on their views," Cuffe said. "Like most people in Leinster House you get on with whoever you have to spend time with, whether they're your arch enemy or your closest friend. The nature of the Oireachtas is you spend long hours in committee rooms with people you might not wish to spend time with, you end up at a conference with somebody, so you get on with everybody and Fianna Fáil saw that in ourselves as much as we saw it with them."

An economic crisis on an unprecedented scale had been unfolding for some time, but there was a worrying and inexplicable time lag in the Government's reaction to events, due in part to the fallout from the Mahon tribunal. Before the realisation hit, a shock humiliation was on the cards for the Government in the form of the result of the first Lisbon Treaty referendum. In a radical departure from their refusenik past, Green TDs and Senators had committed on 15 January 2008 to campaigning for a 'Yes' vote on the Lisbon Treaty, despite having pressed for a 'No' in five EU referendums over the previous 21 years. The ever-democratic Greens could not simply leave the decision to elected parliamentarians, however, and a special party members' convention on the issue was scheduled for the following Saturday in Dublin, with Patricia McKenna popping up again to urge delegates to back a 'No' vote. There was embarrassment when the Green leadership failed to garnish the required two-thirds majority by an unlucky total of 13 votes. It was a hint that many grassroots members perceived the party leadership was already drifting in a different direction from the path they wanted to follow, but Gormley and others chose to interpret the 63 to 37 per cent vote in favour of the treaty as a mandate to recommend a 'Yes' vote. The Greens then found themselves under attack from both the pro- and anti-sides of the debate, with the Labour Party claiming the junior coalition partner had put a 'Yes' vote in jeopardy and Sinn Féin mischievously suggesting 'No' voters within the Green Party should join their camp for the duration of the campaign.

Ryan said "not getting Lisbon debated properly" was one of the biggest mistakes the Fianna Fáil-Green Government ever made. If that was the case, the Greens contributed to that mistake, thanks to their painstaking attachment to grassroots consultation. And although fellow travellers on the 'Yes' side, Fine Gael and Labour, also failed to deliver, Cowen blundered spectacularly badly during the campaign by saying he had not read the treaty from cover to cover. This was a particularly bizarre comment given that he had in fact been deeply involved in the negotiation of the text and knew it back to front. Mortifyingly for Cowen, his rallying cry for the once-famed Fianna Fáil organisation to mobilise in order to get the treaty passed was not even remotely heeded by the Soldiers of Destiny. Ahern, preoccupied with the tribunal, had dithered about setting a date for the referendum, meaning the 'Yes' side's botched campaign got started too late. When it did finally get underway, the 'Yes' campaign was executed with very little passion, while the 'No' campaign was so successful that it even managed to briefly unite the forces of Sinn Féin and the British tabloid press.

And so it came to pass that little more than a month after the unfortunate Cowen took charge of the country he suffered a stunning defeat by the electorate. Irish voters rejected the treaty in June by a decisive margin of 53.4 per cent to 46.6 per cent, with 752,451 people voting 'Yes' and 862,415 opting for a 'No'. The unexpected result provoked a crisis in the European Union, with Libertas leader and prominent Irish 'No' campaigner Declan Ganley describing the result as "brilliant." Even the bookmakers ran out of luck on that Friday 13th, although opinion polls had presented ominous warnings in terms of identifying large numbers of undecided voters.

Cowen was left reeling from the referendum result, which immediately and seriously undermined his authority as Taoiseach, and around the same time he was finally hit with the terrifyingly speedy deterioration in the state of the economy. The Economic and Social Research Institute (ESRI) issued a stark warning that Ireland was heading for recession. Meanwhile, Lenihan told a construction industry conference that the State's building boom, a giddy and ill-advised love affair with property ongoing since the mid-1990s, was coming to a "shuddering end" and the situation was being exacerbated by an international credit crunch. In ad-libbed remarks, Lenihan went on to complain in a light-hearted manner about having had "the misfortune" to be appointed Minister for Finance just a few weeks previously. Bad news about the economy continued to flow non-stop that summer. On July 2, exchequer returns for first half of the year showed a projected €3 billion shortfall in tax revenue. Two days later, Central Statistics Office figures revealed that the number of people claiming unemployment had risen by 10,000 the previous month. On 8 July, Lenihan announced cutbacks of €1.44 billion over two years, with the main element of the plan being a reduction of three per cent in the public payroll. And then in August, Department of Finance figures showed a further €776 million shortfall in July's projected tax revenue.

Cowen, despite his extensive Ministerial experience in the Department of Finance and elsewhere, appeared despondent and not a little bewildered. On a personal level, as someone for whom patriotism was undoubtedly hugely important, he was perhaps beginning to grapple with the reality of his own role in the downturn. He had been inextricably involved in the formulation of policies that had contributed to the scale of the crisis. Serving as Minister for Finance since 2004 until his promotion, he oversaw an unsustainable increase in public spending. More importantly, he did not intervene in an out-of-control property market which was helter-skeltering towards a bust. With the trend for light-touch regulation, the banks had been more or less left to their own devices. Cuffe has subsequently attempted to explain Cowen's delay in absorbing the seriousness of what was coming down the tracks. "I always think that when it comes to fundamental differences between the Greens and Fianna Fáil, the Greens have always had to work really hard and push really hard to be noticed and to effect change. I think if you're immersed within the political culture of one of the larger parties, you can reach a high position in Cabinet without ever having to stick your neck out or have to take a controversial position on any issue. That would be anathema to the Greens. We are well used to robust criticism of almost anything that we do, so I think it was easy for senior figures within Fianna Fáil to say, 'Oh things are fine, things are grand, we'll work through this. There's no need for radical change.' Ironically, the Greens have always argued for radical change in a number of different areas. So I say that by way of understanding maybe the time lag in Brian Cowen's reaction to the unfolding crisis."

When they were in Opposition, the Greens had certainly

railed against the policies that would go on to lead the country to the brink of economic catastrophe. Ryan recalled the dismissive attitude displayed by bankers towards the party pre-2007. "I had already had a lot of discussions back in 2005, 2006. I would have been talking to some of the bank people, the chief executives of the banks. We went into the Irish Bankers Federation as much as anything else because we realised we may be going into Government and they wanted to talk to us and we wanted to talk to them," he said. "We went in saying we thought that mortgage lending was completely out of hand and the lending was gone awry. We were told we didn't understand the markets, we didn't see the fundamentals."

Yet now the Greens were in power when the domestic economy broke like a dam under pressure, and were part of the administration that scrambled to pull together a package of measures designed not only to drastically rein in public spending in the second half of the year but also to present the appearance of something like a semblance of control over the situation. While the slump coincided with a crisis in the banking sector worldwide, the Irish banking system was quickly plunged into a particularly serious situation with collapsing share prices, although the true extent of the problems in this most opaque of sectors would not be revealed for some time. After the collapse of the Wall Street giant Lehman Brothers, talk quickly turned to a blanket banking guarantee lest the entire Irish banking system begin to topple. Anglo Irish Bank was by now in danger of imminent collapse and

AIB and Bank of Ireland were also facing into serious funding difficulties. Gormley said: "The problem with the economy is we weren't getting the facts from the banks. They were just spinning us and people need to understand that the banks are congenitally incapable of telling the truth. That's the problem."

On Thursday 18 September, a furious Lenihan telephoned RTÉ director general Cathal Goan after hearing callers to Joe Duffy's *Liveline* radio programme express concern about the security of their bank accounts. The Minister for Communications was, of course, Ryan, who was not tipped off about Lenihan's direct intervention.

"My sense was it wasn't inappropriate," he said. The State was in a much weakened position, and Lenihan was of the view that the commentary could create a run on the banks. "In fairness we were in the middle of a real crisis ... the programme in particular was not helping and I think it was valid for a minister for finance to talk," he added.

The economist and journalist David McWilliams began to impress upon Gormley his belief that some manner of a guarantee was essential in a prolonged series of text messages to the Green leaders' phone, Ryan remembered, so much so that a guarantee became known as "the McWilliams option" among the Green leadership.

"David McWilliams in particular had been in contact with John Gormley quite extensively in that period ... and I know David had been advising John in terms of saying we had to do a guarantee, we had to put that in place." Boyle believed McWilliams started lobbying Gormley long before the celebrity economist's well-documented late-night visit from Lenihan on 17 September, during which McWilliams claimed to have recommended a guarantee on bank deposits and funding but not on subordinated debt.

"John in either Cabinet meetings or outside Cabinet meetings would have been very big at pushing the bank guarantee, David McWilliams would have gone to him first," Boyle said.

Following a crisis meeting in Government Buildings on the night of 29 September, Cowen and Lenihan, in consultation with officials, senior bankers and others, decided to guarantee all deposits and the bulk of other liabilities in the six Irish banks and building societies: AIB, Bank of Ireland, Anglo, Irish Life & Permanent, EBS and Irish Nationwide. This was estimated as totalling €440 billion of liabilities. Other Cabinet Ministers were required to approve the measure, but Gormley was asleep and could not be contacted by officials who were trying to call him in the very early hours of the morning. While Irish politicians have traditionally tended to burn the candle at both ends, Gormley placed a strong emphasis on the value of a good night's sleep and was known to retire early. Gormley was eventually woken by a Garda at his door asking him to ring the Taoiseach's office as a matter of urgency. The Green leader subsequently faced some level of ridicule for this, but Boyle continues to defend Gormley strongly. "I mean what else would John be doing at two o'clock in the morning but sleeping? ... It wouldn't have changed a damn thing." The need for the decision had already been established, all that remained necessary was a formal rubber-stamp to ensure the legitimacy of the decision was confirmed once the scope of the guarantee had been determined, Boyle argued. However, the scope of the guarantee would become the contentious element of the deal. Boyle insisted a "huge mythology" later grew up around the difficulty contacting Gormley. "The Cabinet in effect had already decided that the policy to be followed was the bank guarantee. What determined it then was the timing and to what scope. That's what the meeting in Government Buildings was that night. That was a Finance meeting that Brian Cowen attended with the heads of the banks. It wasn't a Cabinet meeting. It was in the middle of the night," Boyle said. "The markets were opening at 9 o'clock the following morning so they had what was called an incorporeal Cabinet meeting ... It means that people are consulted without physically being in the same room ... or physically called to as in John's case."

By his own admission, however, Ryan was not centrally involved in the formulation of the guarantee, although Gormley kept him "in the loop" in the week running up to it. Afterwards he resolved to move closer to the situation even though his Ministry did not have fiscal responsibility. "After that I suppose I had a personal sense that I needed to get closer to it to understand it, not to be just caught by surprise in a sense by developments, so I would have made it my business ... to kind of try to talk to

Brian Lenihan, talk to other people, to try to get a sense of what was going on," he said. In the period between the bank guarantee and the establishment of the National Asset Management Agency (Nama), Ryan was at odds with his senior Government colleagues. "My personal view at the time was saying we should have gone and nationalised all the banks," he said.

According to Trevor Sargent, "Armageddon" was seen as the only possible outcome if such a wide guarantee was not granted, and quickly. He said the matter was kept very much within the upper echelons of Cabinet, "and the breaking of the news was on the media for me." He remembered hearing the item on early morning radio with a sense of disbelief, "because I would have expected probably to be more in the loop or to have some inkling of it." Up until then Sargent said he had simply been given the official line that the fundamentals of the economy were sound and the banks were well capitalised. The opinion of the Greens on the implications of the guarantee was not sought, he said. "I wouldn't say [it was] discussed. It was presented as we have no choice in this matter if we want to be able to get money out of ATM machines and pay nurses and gardai and teachers and the civil service and dole and pensions and everything else."

Sargent continued: "It happened so quickly that it was presented as the only responsible thing to do was to do this and to do it quickly. To think there was any other option was to delude ourselves ... potential Armageddon [was] seen as the option."

Paul Gogarty identified this hectic and confusing period as

the time when Green ideology was finally confronted with real-politik, and the party's TDs at last understood the true and painful difference between being politicians in power as opposed to critics on the sideline in Opposition. "There was a moral obligation to make decisions that were counter-intuitive to us," Gogarty said. He was also honest enough to admit that, if the Greens had not entered Government in 2007, they might have adopted a similar stance to the one espoused by some Opposition politicians at the time. "This is what really pisses me off about the Shinners [Sinn Féin] and the Socialist Workers. If you did what they were saying you wouldn't have the rich paying for it, because the rich would have departed the country, you'd have the ordinary people paying for it. I mean it's a false argument. If they don't know that they're delusional. But then again, to be fair, we might have been saying the same thing and it's only from being in Government that you actually face the reality and make a decision based on what's true rather than what you'd like it to be."

There was a staggering lack of economic expertise in Leinster House in 2008. Traditional occupations dominated, with the established parties in the Oireachtas populated mostly by former schoolteachers, small-town solicitors, farmers, auctioneers and publicans. The Green TDs were equally unqualified to handle the financial meltdown, with their schooling in economics little better than that of their counterparts in other parties. Although his background was in community youth work, Boyle appeared have a decent grasp of the economic situation and was the party's finance spokesman. Ryan held a Bachelor of Commerce degree from University College Dublin and had some contacts in the banking sector thanks in part to the fact that his father was a former banker who would have been on friendly terms with Michael Somers, then the chief executive of the National Treasury Management Agency.

The Budget unveiled in October 2008, provoked controversy about the over-70s' medical card and unleashed a wave of public anger, as well as internal dissent within the Green Party. The Green leadership was forced to defend the party's decision to support cutbacks in the education sector and increased class sizes, which was new and extremely uncomfortable territory. Gormley denied there was a rift in the party, but councillors were talking openly about their discomfort in continuing in the Coalition were Bronwen Maher from Dublin, Chris O'Leary from Cork and Clare's Brian Meaney. A town councillor, Betty Doran from Mullingar in Co. Westmeath, had already announced she was resigning from the party in protest at the Budget. Measures that had been announced were reversed – the plan to abolish the medical card for the over-70s was changed and the one per cent income level amended to exempt those earning the minimum wage. But party members were beginning to wonder just what the party's bottom line actually was. Boyle described the Budget as "traumatic" and said it had a huge effect on the party in the local and European elections the following year.

Mary White said public opinion began to turn against the Greens almost as soon as the economic crisis struck, making it hard for the party to get its environmental agenda and other policy targets off the starting blocks.

"[It was] as if by being in Government that we were imposing this pain and horrendous number of budgets and the cataclysmic banking disaster that was imploding all around us, that we were the reason that that was happening. And I don't think there was a logical connection between what people were thinking about the Greens personally and their own personal grief about what was happening to them in terms of losing their jobs or losing their savings or whatever. They just saw us as propping up Fianna Fáil. And if you took away the prop everything would be OK, which of course is a very fallacious argument," White said. Thoughts of withdrawing from Government naturally flitted across the minds of the Green deputies but were dismissed just as quickly. "We would've been accused then of being the flaky Greens who couldn't hack it," White continued. Making an effort to stabilise the situation seemed a more honourable option. "People with any logical perspective would have seen that we were in for the first time, we didn't carry any baggage, we were doing our honest to God best every single day that we were in there, but we became the whipping boy or girl for Fianna Fáil." But White and her colleagues would soon discover such arguments held no resonance for the electorate, "and we became absolutely the personification of everything that was wrong in the country."

CHAPTER 5

A TASTE OF WHAT WAS TO COME

DAN BOYLE WAS RUNNING IN THE EUROPEAN ELECTIONS FOR THE party, but by the time May 2009 rolled around he believed his campaign was going so badly that he had pretty much written off his chances of ever making it as an MEP. So he floated what was then a novel idea among colleagues in the parliamentary party of using Twitter to publicise a speech he was going to make in Tralee, Co. Kerry. Not only was he going to be critical of Government policy in the speech, but he was also going to demand a review of the Programme for Government on behalf of the Greens. Some of his colleagues were sceptical, particularly about his new means of publicising the content, but they came around to the notion eventually. "I must admit there was a reluctant agreement," he said.

To observers of politics, Boyle's plan walked, talked and looked like an exit strategy from the Coalition Government. He claimed that most of the Green Party elements of the Programme for Government had already been implemented, and the greatly changed economic circumstances now meant that a renegotiation of the agreement was a no-brainer. The Greens cited planning regulations and new insulation and energy targets as achievements of which they were particularly proud, along with a Government commitment to bring in a directly-elected mayor of Dublin – a largely unwanted piece of legislation with which the party would develop something close to an irrational fixation. Those who had been encouraged to give their votes to the Greens for the first time in 2007, but more especially those who had stuck with the party through the lean years, could be forgiven for asking, 'Is that all there is?' The Greens' call for a renegotiation was a clumsy attempt to quickly put some kind of distance between themselves and Fianna Fáil, which was becoming increasingly unpopular under Brian Cowen, on the eve of the local and European elections. Cowen's jaded and morose demeanour was doing both Coalition parties no favours at all. His extreme shyness and apparent self-consciousness about his burly appearance regularly manifested itself as sullenness and a seeming disregard for neat presentation. Staff regularly presented him with carefully thought-out plans that would allow the desk-bound Taoiseach to reach out to people on trips around the country, while also incorporating manageable media appearances. But when it came to modern political communications, Cowen was like a serial dieter who would grasp hold of the latest fad with feverish enthusiasm, only to drop it within weeks and revert stubbornly to negative old habits. The Greens went to the other extreme, over-saturating the airwaves by popping up on nearly every radio programme and providing a party spokesperson for each television news slot. The electorate would not thank them for their availability; the Green talking heads merely put themselves even more in the firing line of angry voters.

The Green Party's director of elections Mary White stressed the importance of a positive attitude in the face of adversity in a message to the party faithful in the Green Voice newsletter, in which she claimed to be upbeat about candidates' chances of success. "There is a lot of doom and gloom out there. We need to cut through it with our Green Party optimism," White chirruped. "We know the economy is in poor shape. But we have the tools and policies to make it better," she claimed. Despite such cheery mentoring, the electorate would round on the Greens in the local and European elections with a severity that shocked both the party's base and its leadership. The party's two Euro candidates, Boyle and Deirdre de Burca, put on a poor show. Boyle got only 15,499 first preference votes in Ireland South, where Fianna Fáil's Brian Crowley, Fine Gael's Sean Kelly and Alan Kelly of Labour were elected MEPs. De Burca, who ran in the Dublin constituency, was humiliated after coming in behind Patricia McKenna, who had put herself forward as an Independent. McKenna had left the party in May 2009, accusing the Greens of "selling out" – a common complaint among those who departed the party. Gay Mitchell of Fine Gael, Proinsias de Rossa of Labour and the Socialist Joe Higgins were successful in Dublin, with de Burca trailing in their wake after securing just 19,086 votes. The party's representatives in the two Dublin by-elections – Elizabeth Davidson in Dublin

South and David Geary in Dublin Central – also sank without trace. The death of Fianna Fáil's Seamus Brennan in July of the previous year had created a Dáil vacancy in Dublin South, which was filled by RTÉ's former economics editor George Lee, with an incredible 27,768 votes. Lee would only dip his toe into politics for a brief period as a Fine Gael TD before resigning his seat in February 2010, however. Independent Maureen O'Sullivan reaped the spoils in Dublin Central, where she had been the late Tony Gregory's director of elections.

The Greens went into the local elections with 15 councillors and emerged with a paltry three, making it practically impossible to keep Green issues anywhere close to the top of local government's agenda. The only survivors at council level were Brian Meaney in Clare and Malcolm Noonan in Kilkenny, with just one newcomer squeezing through: Mark Dearey, who won a seat on Louth County Council having previously been a borough councillor in Dundalk. Even in Dublin, where the Greens had always been able to count on a decent amount of middle-class support, all eight council seats were lost. It was an ominous sign of what was to come in the General Election. The Greens had banked on the electorate factoring in that the party had not been in power when the seeds of economic disaster were planted. It either failed to anticipate or greatly underestimated the wrath of furious voters.

In the same month, the put-upon Greens discovered they had inadvertently made an enemy of the outspoken motor retailer Bill Cullen, star of TV3's The Apprentice programme. Changes to the VRT system linking the levels of tax to CO_2 emission had "killed the motor trade", Cullen claimed. It was all the Greens fault, he insisted.

By this stage, the Greens had already been hit with a number of troubling resignations. McKenna had become a thorn in the side of the party leadership and they were not sorry to see her go. Councillor Chris O'Leary, the only Green on Cork City Council, had announced he was leaving the party in January because of what he described as a "stay in government at all costs" agenda. He retained his seat as an Independent councillor, and went on to join Sinn Féin. In Dublin, Bronwen Maher resigned from the Greens citing "irreconcilable differences" she had with the direction in which the leadership was guiding the party. She went on to join the Labour Party. The situation was not good in Donegal either, where Neil Clarke had resigned from the party and Letterkenny Town Council in December 2008, saying he had become disillusioned and could not go before the voters again as a Green.

A number of defections from the Fianna Fáil party had left the Government in a precarious position and it could no longer be certain of a majority in Dáil votes without strict enforcement of attendance in the chamber. In theory, this should have benefited the Greens. Negotiations to revise the Programme for Government got underway at the end of September, shortly before the second vote on the Lisbon Treaty referendum, which passed this time. Eamon Ryan believed the Greens were right to reconsider the Programme for Government, but acknowledged that the wider public did not take too kindly to the idea. "I think that the public didn't like it. They had a slight sense that maybe here's a party that actually two years ago, or a year and a half, went into Government and wasn't needed and now is needed and is using that to deliver a whole range of programme stuff that doesn't address the whole fundamental issue that everyone's concerned about, which was the immediate banking crisis," he said. "But I actually think again even if it didn't sit well publicly or politically with the wider public, it was the right thing to do." Ryan said Irish politics and the wider world had changed so much, particularly in the economic sphere, during the Green's relatively brief period in office that it was correct that the Government should reassess its Programme as part of its response to the financial crisis. It was also a useful preview of what would have to be done at the next Budget, he said. The renewed programme was generally viewed as a negotiating success for the Greens at the time, although it would be shown to have restricted the Coalition's budgetary options to some extent.

Burned by their first experience of attempting to negotiate a programme, the Greens were much better prepared second time around. The Green negotiators were Ryan, Boyle and Mary White. "Eamon was playing the good cop, Dan was playing the bad cop and I was just being myself," White said. On the Fianna Fáil team this time were Mary Hanafin, the Minister for Social and Family Affairs, the Justice Minister Dermot Ahern and the ultra-efficient Minister for Transport Noel Dempsey, fountain pen and piles of files at the ready. It was obvious from the minute they began meeting on the last day of September that the Greens had upped their game, presenting more than 260 proposals. White recalled the Greens marched into the first meeting with detailed documents, while Fianna Fáil "had nothing." Donall Geoghegan had a similar recollection. "I remember the main thing from that negotiation, which we had prepared very well for, the main thing was that Fianna Fáil had no agenda. I really mean now they had nothing." The Fianna Fáil delegation returned the following day with something they had "cobbled together", White claimed. "I think they suddenly realised we were deadly serious," she said. "We were absolutely intent and serious about this deal because we had to sell it to our members. We had to vote on it. We had to get two thirds, and we also had to vote on Nama at the same time."

Tensions flared between Hanafin and White at one point. "Mary Hanafin said the Greens are only interested in bikes, bulbs and bunnies. And I said back to her, *sotto voce*, you're only interested in bankers, builders and bailouts. I was so pleased with myself," she laughed.

Geoghegan believed that may have been the very day Hanafin briefed the American Ambassador about her true feelings on the Greens. "I think I remember that day. We finished early … and I said, 'What's going on?' and she said 'I've to go to the American Embassy', or something like that." Overall, Geoghegan was pleased with what the Greens achieved in the negotiation, admitting that they had not done too well at all in 2007. "We pushed hard and we got a much better deal in that programme than we'd done in the first one. I wouldn't be particularly proud to be honest of the first programme for Government. I don't think it was that great at all, lots of disappointing things in it, but the renegotiated programme for Government was much more progressive." The deal incorporated electoral reform and changes to the law around political donations; a review of TDs expenses and travel allowances and new expense guidelines for Ministers, and the elimination of what the Greens believed were "unnecessary" tax reliefs. But it was the educational reforms that the Greens were most keen to highlight.

The thorny topic of education had been left until the very end of the negotiations because both sides knew it would be contentious. It was left so late that the agreed proposals barely made it into the document that was brought to the RDS to be presented to Green delegates as they arrived. Paul Gogarty had dug his heels in and threatened to walk if he did not get exactly what he wanted, ensuring that the Greens effectively vetoed any new student charges. Gogarty also demanded that education cuts imposed in the last Budget be reversed. A key requirement was the restoration of the pupil-teacher ratio from one to 28 back to one to 27 in primary schools. He was facing opposition not only from Fianna Fáil but within his own party on the issue. "I had to fight even within the Green Party to do that ... Most people didn't see the benefit of pushing education so strongly. They were saying, 'Where's the money coming from?'" Gogarty had resigned as the party's education spokesman in March, saying he had been undermined by a decision taken at a party conference to set up a group tasked with achieving the Green's education commitments. He was quietly re-appointed at the end of October.

Gogarty was briefing White, who was dealing with Education in the negotiations. White felt that the party got a good deal on education in the end. "I was well briefed by Paul that this was what we had to get and we got it, but it wasn't without brinkmanship, standing on the precipice looking into the void." However, Ryan later claimed the changes designed to protect education were in reality of no political benefit to the Greens, because soon the Government would be "cutting teachers pay and cutting parents' income." The Minister for Education, Batt O'Keeffe, had made no secret of his support for a system of student loans and continued to refuse to rule out an increase in registration fees.

Cowen and Gormley met briefly to rubber-stamp the new deal. During their meeting, according to a source close to the discussions, Cowen popped his head out of the door and told his staff he needed a car for the Áras in 15 minutes time. He closed the door briefly before opening it again with a 'gotcha'-type laugh in the directly of astonished staffers. The new programme was approved by an 84 per cent majority at a meeting in the RDS on Saturday 10 October and the Greens were flushed with success. But, in retrospect, Boyle found that the entire exercise counter-productive. "Because of the economic circumstances we allowed a narrative to develop that while we were achieving significantly in terms of policies, and would have achieved more had it [the Government] run full term, we were letting others to allow us to be perceived as being preoccupied with minor issues and not being concerned with the wider issue, when there was so much of our energy going into the wider issue," Boyle said.

The wider issue was of course the economic situation, which continued to dominate. The ever-optimistic Ryan allowed himself to believe at this point that the future was looking a little brighter as he reflected on the Government's economic approach as 2009 turned into 2010. "That I think was the right approach and I think, to a certain extent, it was working in 2010. If you look at the market commentary, if you look at the economy, there was a certain return of activity, there was international confidence coming back, bond prices came down. It was starting to work," Ryan said. "I mean, I wouldn't be that blind to read everything into two or three months economic data but it was a certain sense – and particularly a lot of comment that the Irish were getting their budget in order – that the economy was starting to turn."

At its first meeting after the 2009 Easter break, the Cabinet had signed-off on legislation establishing a State agency tasked with buying toxic property investment loans from the banks. It would be called the National Asset Management Agency, or Nama for short, and was essentially the brainchild of economist Peter Bacon. And it stuck in the craw of a large number of Green Party supporters. While the book value of the loans was estimated at €90 billion, Boyle and others believed Nama should seek a discount of at least 50 per cent when buying the loans and transferring them from the ownership of the banks to the State. He argued the banks had over-valued the loans to limit their exposure. Opposition finance spokespeople, Richard Bruton of Fine Gael and Joan Burton of Labour, pointed out a discount of this size would require new State capital to offset the inevitable large losses, landing the Government in a majority shareholding position in some instances.

Nama was being created under the aegis of the National Treasury Management Agency (NTMA), which was soon inundated with CVs from out of work accountants, tax specialists, lawyers and bankers. Addressing the Irish Planning Institute's annual conference in Wexford, Ryan said unsustainable lending by banks had left Ireland in a tangled mess. He conceded the approach to tackling the crisis was neither flawless, nor without risk, but insisted it was not meant to rescue delinquent developers but rather serve the public interest. The Greens pronounced themselves keen to ensure developers who defaulted on property loans should be prevented by law from buying them back again at lower prices, and argued Nama should also deliver lands for public housing in time to come.

Ryan recalled the first time he got his head around the Nama concept, having been brought in for a lunch in the NTMA shortly after Minister for Finance Brian Lenihan commissioned Bacon to do an assessment of the various different options available. Among those present and discussing the immediate crisis were Bacon himself; NTMA chief executive Michael Somers and John Corrigan, director of the National Pensions Reserve Fund who would replace Somers when he stepped down later that year;

Brendan McDonagh, an NTMA director and soon to be Nama managing director. "The clear sense of that meeting was that urgently we needed to do something like what turns out to be Nama. We needed an asset management system to be able to go to the European central bank and get liquidity from the assets," Ryan said. "The sense that there was an urgency there of being quick and of being honest in terms of assessing what the losses were. And a very strong sense that this is going to be a large scale, this isn't going to be a five or ten billion, it's going to be a multiples billion asset purchase which is going to be discounted dramatically which is going to allow us to maintain a liquidity position that avoids banks shutting down. That was the first time that I had I suppose the concept, of rather than nationalising the banks, using an asset management vehicle to do it." Ryan thought the plan was high risk but, with a little tweaking, would prove the best of the options on the table at that time. Now he had to persuade the Green grassroots to think the same way because some party members were very concerned about the plan, "perfectly understandably."

Given the Greens democratic tradition, the legislation to enact Nama could not be passed until the support from party membership was secured. There was dissent on the Nama issue, but those opposed to the policy needed to attract two-thirds support if the party was to officially reject the Government's preferred approach. Ahead of the vote in the RDS which also approved the renewed Programme for Government, a motion opposing the setting up of Nama was rejected by a large majority. The motion had been phrased in a negative way, meaning the anti-Nama wing had to garner 66 per cent of the vote. In the event they managed 31 per cent, with 69 per cent siding with the leadership. Some delegates felt a gun had been put to their head. Boyle frankly admitted that the backing for Nama in the RDS was motivated by the realisation that if it was not passed the party would be out of Government, combined with the fact that a genuinely-improved – from a Green perspective – Programme for Government was on the table at the same time.

Boyle said while Nama was necessary, it damaged the party politically, both inside and out, because, as a concept, it developed a "totemic" quality.

"The unfortunate thing about Nama was the damage it did within the party because it got a totemic quality about it. And in reality Nama, or a version of Nama, would've had to have happened anyway. It was seen to be the root of all evil. It was seen to be an effort to protect Fianna Fáil backers, protect the banks and protect the developers, when in fact it was a tool that had to be availed of. You had to get rid of bad bank loans. It was the element of the equation that there should have been least concern about, but there was most preoccupation … Of itself it developed this quality that did cause a lot of damage within the party."

However, Boyle was happy about the Greens involvement in the establishment of Nama, which marked a departure from the party's lack of genuine participation in previous economic matters, and he felt Green demands about the Nama Bill and board membership were listened to. At the time, the Green leadership argued that the internal debate within the party on Nama would contribute to the Government and the Irish people getting better legislation on the asset recovery plan. But Ryan later perceived that the whole episode had once again played badly with the wider public. "I think the public disliked that. I think that resonated very badly with the Irish public who said, 'Why is it that this group of people are having a vote and having a say?'" While the Greens were patting themselves on the back for being so democratic, those on the outside looking in were far from impressed. "I think it did it a certain amount of damage politically in the sense of, 'How come it's the Green party members [who] are deciding national stuff?'"

And yet Ryan said he would go through the same process with Nama again, because he believed it was the right thing to do. "My personal perspective is that's our democratic tradition, it is one of the decision being made by a large number of people is better than one being made by a small number of people," he said. "The changes that we made because of including people were positive ones and ultimately that's our political approach and I think it's a good one. I think it strengthens you rather than weakens you. And I think that even if it was frustrating for others that we took some time or we were seen to have influence that some people didn't like, but actually I think that was absolutely the right thing to do in my mind. It was difficult in the party internally but I'm very glad that we engaged in that sort of process."

This kind of democratic engagement with party grassroots

did not concern the Green's partners in Government, Fianna Fáil, Ryan noted. He was struck by stylistic differences between the coalition partners when it came to delegating responsibility for economic matters. "The way Fianna Fáil works is that ... it's quite a hierarchical organisation so if you've got a Minister for Finance that's his responsibility. We work in a rather different way and we would be going back to the Green parliamentary party as well as to the membership on a regular basis," he said. "We're characterised by being fairly fair and open; in their discussions they're characterised by being more hierarchical. I think ultimately they had a sense that Brian Lenihan had a better call on it than Joan Burton or Richard Bruton and they put their trust in him."

Ryan acknowledged that the Government made many mistakes before and after that autumn, but recalled that particular period as a good one. He said "only time will tell" if Nama was the correct approach. "It'll depend how it works over the next five years but in my mind, and I think in the assessment of others ... I don't know what other alternative would have worked." He admitted it took too long to get the administration of Nama up and running, and faced criticism that the delay and uncertainty about evaluations damaged public confidence in the process as well as international confidence in Ireland. However, he concluded: "I think the process and the approach was a valid one." Prior to the RDS event, Boyle said the leadership made every effort to inform members about the contentious plan. There were a series of meetings at the Hilton Hotel overlooking the Grand Canal in Dublin, where Lenihan's trusted special adviser Dr Alan Ahearne, an economics lecturer from NUI Galway, was invited to brief the Greens. Invitations were extended to a number of others, who had earned or were in the process of earning, the title 'celebrity economist', including Constantin Gurdgiev and Brian Lucey. Geoghegan recalled the birth of the Nama concept as a difficult time for the Greens but something which, he thought, allowed for an useful engagement with members and activists. He too recalled the lively debates in the Hilton and the vote in the RDS was, he felt, "extraordinary really for a political party." In contrast to Ryan, Geoghegan argued that internal debate within the Green Party "kind of played out then in the public consciousness." He continued: "In effect what we did was we took that uneasiness with what Nama was and was going to be and made it into a kind of a drama with in the Green Party ... having an internal debate that was much bigger than us and involved the Irish electorate, second hand but in a way." It was a trick that could not be pulled too often, however. "You can't do Government by special convention," he acknowledged.

Hostility within the party, and outside, to the idea of Nama remained. The Greens also attempted to flag a policy concept they dubbed 'My Nama', but it received little traction, although the idea of an expert group designed to help those struggling with personal and mortgage debt was a sound one.

In November it emerged that the Greens would be entitled to fill a vacancy in the Seanad caused by the election of Labour's Alan Kelly to the European Parliament in June. Party whips from

Fianna Fáil and the Greens had agreed on alternating replacements for vacancies on non-Government seats. Niall Ó Brolcháin, the former mayor of Galway who had called for Bertie Ahern to resign, would get the nod to join his colleagues Boyle and Deirdre de Burca in the Upper House.

CHAPTER 6

'F*** YOU DEPUTY STAGG'

PAUL GOGARTY WAS BEING HECKLED IN THE DÁIL CHAMBER ONE tense winter afternoon when he turned on the Labour Party's Emmet Stagg and spat out the venomous words: "With all due respect, in the most unparliamentary language, fuck you Deputy Stagg. Fuck you."

Mary White, who had been keeping an eye on the debate by using the monitor in her Dáil office, clapped her hand over her mouth and rushed up the corridor, in the modern wing of Leinster House known as LH2000, to Ciaran Cuffe's room, crying: "Have you heard Paul?" The pair were flabbergasted. "We couldn't believe it," she said, "and then of course it was all around the world in seconds." There would be no way for the Greens' communications experts to contain this particular controversy, as a clip of the snarling party TD went viral on YouTube, and was broadcast across the globe almost instantly. "I think it was one of those moments: where were you when Paul effed and blinded?" White said.

Emotions had been running high on 11 December, 2009

when a painful Social Welfare Bill that legislated for cuts of some €760 million the following year was being debated. Pushing through the cutbacks was the then Minister for Social and Family Affairs Mary Hanafin, who said while the Government was reducing social welfare payments with "a very heavy heart" it was something that had to be done because of the increasing severity of the economic situation. Later, Gogarty was challenged by exasperated Opposition TDs in a sparsely populated chamber to vote with his conscience and against the Bill, which would go on to pass all stages in the Dáil that night with the Government winning by 81 to 75 votes.

Ahead of his outburst, Gogarty had been claiming that the Green party had succeeded in getting the size of the social welfare cuts reduced. Tellingly, he admitted that if he was sitting across the chamber on the Opposition benches, perhaps without access to figures revealing the true state of the country's finances, he too would be "clamouring for blood." He as good as denounced his Government's proposed legislation, adding: "It would be highly disingenuous of me and totally insincere, therefore, to say anything other than that this is a grossly unfair section and that the Bill is grossly unfair." As he continued to speak, and defend his support for the Bill although apparently unable to justify the unjustifiable, he was heckled by Labour Party TDs. Gogarty snapped. Rounding on Stagg in particular, he said: "With all due respect, in the most unparliamentary language, fuck you Deputy Stagg. Fuck you." He immediately apologised for his intemperate use of language, and withdrew the remarks, adding however that he was outraged that anyone would question his sincerity.

Michael Kennedy of Fianna Fáil, who had been presiding over the proceedings as acting chairman, was reduced to stuttering: "Hey. Excuse me, Deputy Gogarty, that is most unparliamentary language." After a break in proceedings called in order to restore decorum to a chamber by now in disarray, Gogarty delivered what Lucinda Creighton of Fine Gael described as a "half-hearted, mealy-mouthed apology" that displayed an unprecedented level of arrogance and contempt for colleagues in the national parliament. The Green TD had, in the meantime, consulted the document that was used to decide what constituted unparliamentary language during Dáil sittings, with its quaint title of 'Salient Rulings of the House', and discovered his insult of choice was not one of the forbidden expressions. The official list of banned words included: brat; buffoon; chancer; communist; corner boy; coward; fascist; gurrier; guttersnipe; hypocrite; rat; scumbag; scurrilous and yahoo. Insinuations of drunkenness against a fellow member were also out of order, the rulings made clear. However, "fuck you", while obviously not encouraged, was nevertheless not singled out as unacceptable – as Gogarty rather tenuously pointed out, much to the irritation of Opposition deputies. "Under the salient rulings of the Chair, No. 428, the terminology I used was not included in the list," he bleated. "However, No. 431 rules that political charges are in order but personal charges will not be made," he said. "Members must not be thin-skinned in relation to political remarks. I was thin-skinned and I should not have used unparliamentary language and I apologise profusely to the House."

Speaking outside the chamber in the immediate aftermath of the outburst, a somewhat giddy Gogarty insisted his participation in the heated exchanges was a "genuine emotive response" to having his integrity questioned by another deputy, although he could not even recall exactly what Stagg had said to upset him quite so much. Gogarty said he had always been a straight talker, although he acknowledged words like the one he had adopted should not be used in parliament. Demonstrating that he was not going to lose much sleep over the incident, he threw in a popular culture reference for good measure. "I said it; I apologised for it … it's probably too much to ask for, but I do hope that what I said in my speech will be covered, rather than just the lyrics of a Lily Allen song," he said.

The Dáil record showed Stagg had been needling Gogarty about his "bleating and blather", before saying the Green backbencher "does not seem very sincere." Afterwards Stagg, no stranger to robust arguments, said he was not concerned in the slightest about the personal insult hurled in his direction. It was nothing he had not heard before, albeit in a different setting. Stagg added that he would prefer if journalists in Leinster House and observers outside were to focus on the implications of the Bill that had been under debate, rather than the use of an expletive. "I'm a thick-skinned person and in politics you develop a hide. The use of the four-letter word is inappropriate of course, but I have often been told to you-know-what before," Stagg said. "I'd be very disappointed if Paul Gogarty's misuse of a few words in the house took away from the real news: a really savage Social Welfare Bill."

While most of those who worked in Leinster House felt Gogarty had offended the essential decorum of the place, and brought the wrong kind of attention to Irish politics, visiting groups of schoolchildren were delighted by the sensation the scandal had created and kept their eyes peeled for a sighting of the cursing TD. For any parliamentarian the language was inappropriate, but the vulgarity was totally out of sync with the Green's particularly delicate sensibilities. Eamon Ryan was utterly disgusted and thought Gogarty should be punished severely; John Gormley, who always made allowances for Gogarty's misdemeanours, found the incident mildly embarrassing but not unforgivable in the circumstances. Gormley's political assessment of the situation was that the furore would blow over given that Gogarty had apologised. White remains as shocked as if Gogarty had dropped the expletive only yesterday, however. "I was brought up to be very, very cautious with improper language ... bad language was a no-no in our family, so I find even now ... I can't believe it. I couldn't believe that Paul said it. I remember saying to Paul, 'Why did you say it?' He said, 'It came out.'"

Gogarty continues to insist the outburst should be seen in

the context of what he described as "ongoing assaults", in the form of verbal criticisms of him, from members of the Opposition. He accused Shane McEntee of Fine Gael of playing the national card, as well as tugging on emotional heart-strings, earlier in the debate. McEntee had indeed delivered an emotional contribution, prompted by his engagement with four deaf youngsters he spotted signing to each other behind the pane of glass that cuts the elevated Visitors' Gallery off from the chamber. McEntee's uncle had taught him to sign, so he was able to communicate with the young people briefly from his seat down below. When he sought them out later, one of them asked him a heartbreaking question: was the Minister for Finance going to take money from them? After relating this story, McEntee then gestured dramatically towards the bronze sculptures surrounding the chamber behind the TDs' benches. They were representations of the men who had signed the Proclamation of Independence, promising to cherish all the children of the nation equally. McEntee then zoned in on Gogarty, claiming that while Ministers in the current administration had betrayed those who died in the 1916 Easter Rising, Government backbenchers now had a chance to take a moral stand. "The front bench of the Green Party threw the party away when the Nama Bill came before us. Now it will do the same again. I ask Deputy Gogarty to stand up to it. He knows right from wrong," McEntee cried. This was heavy, emotive stuff, and Gogarty would have been wiser to stay in his office as he was not even required to sit through the debate. But that was not in his confrontational nature. "I just decided to be there," he said. "I didn't have to be there but I just thought: it's a momentous debate; it's an historic debate. I want to be there; I don't want to hide away."

Despite Ryan's strength of feeling on the matter, White confirmed that Gogarty was not reprimanded by his colleagues. "It wasn't a question of reprimanding him. We had a discussion, as the Greens would, a good discussion about it at the next parliamentary party [meeting]." The Greens accepted that Gogarty was suffering from "intense frustration", as indeed many of them were, and decided the best thing to do was to try to put it behind them. There remained the possibility of a reprimand from outside the party, however. Ceann Comhairle Séamus Kirk warned that "decent standards" had to be maintained in Leinster House, and confirmed the incident was being referred to the Dáil Committee on Procedure and Privileges. "It's important we have respect for the House and respect for one another in the House. The important thing is that this doesn't happen again," Kirk intoned. But while the Committee on Procedure and Privileges went on to condemn Gogarty's outburst and said his behaviour had brought the parliament into disrepute, no further action was contemplated.

Fine Gael Senator Frances Fitzgerald, who would go on to be elected in Gogarty's Dublin Mid-West constituency in 2011 and be appointed Minister for Children, could not resist a pointed jibe at Gogarty following his vote in favour of the harsh legislation, however. "If only Paul Gogarty got as upset about careers, blind pensioners and dole recipients as he does about perceived slights to his ego," she said. There was some history between Fitzgerald and Gogarty. He had slumped alarmingly to the floor while she was criticising Gormley during an address to a public meeting in Rathcoole in 2008. Gogarty claimed he had merely been trying to alert the attention of the committee with a series of elaborate gestures – which he was happy to act out for anyone who was interested – because he was annoyed that Fitzgerald had politicised the meeting with her comments. However, he acknowledged one of the commandments of politics applied here: "If you're explaining, you're losing." *The Irish Times* colour writer Miriam Lord was tipped off about the incident and when she called Gogarty he said of Fitzgerald: "She always induces that sort of reaction in me. Hypocrisy and false indignation reverberating from a persona has a damaging effect on my psyche."

The verbal assault on Stagg was of course neither the first nor the last time Gogarty would employed coarse language to explosive effect. Gogarty would find himself in the midst of controversy again at the end of September 2010 after launching a bitter tirade against Labour leader Eamon Gilmore on Twitter. Gogarty claimed Gilmore was being disingenuous by not taking a stand on certain political issues, including the Croke Park deal in which the Government and trade unions agreed industrial peace in return for no redundancies in the public sector. In a tweet, Gogarty dubbed the Labour leader "Gutless Gilmore" and said Gilmore had a "strategy of saying nothing and promising nothing so damned eloquently." Gogarty continued: "Doing the right thing ain't easy, unlike Gutless Gilmore. It's not about the next election - it's about the next generation stupid!" In response to a comment from another Twitter user, he resorted to the old reliable, writing: "I don't give a f*** about Gutless Gilmore." Dan Boyle, also famous for his Twitter battles, said Gogarty went out of his way to be the most provocative member of the party. "He'll admit himself there's no doubt Paul is the most difficult one but he deliberately makes himself provocative. He sees that as his role," Boyle said. Gogarty also gave an expletive-laden interview to *Hot Press* magazine in February 2009, in which he expanded graphically and crudely on the widely-used metaphor that the Greens had got into bed with Fianna Fáil when entering Coalition. "We are lying there bollix naked next to Fianna Fáil. We have been screwed by them a few times, but we are hoping we can roll them around to get what we want, over the longer terms," he explained.

Back in November 2003, he had described the newly-hiked salaries and benefits that TDs were set to enjoy as an "urination" on the less well-off in society who would soon be facing into cutbacks. Shortly afterwards he found himself falling into step on his way towards one of the Leinster House lifts with Ryan. "Some of my constituents didn't like your phraseology there," the mild-mannered Ryan murmured to Gogarty. Gogarty protested at this gentlest of rebukes, claiming he thought his use of the word "urination" had actually been quite reasonable because it portrayed the imagery he wanted to conjure up without resort to foul-mouthed language. Being Gogarty, he expressed himself to

Ryan a little more colourfully, of course. "I said to Eamon, 'Well your constituents can go and fuck themselves, because that's the truth.'" Something of a lull in the conversation ensued as the lift continued its ascent, until Ryan finally spoke. "Well actually it was my father who said that," he said quietly. A cringing Gogarty said "Oh, apologies to your father." But the pair had never really gelled. "Myself and Eamon Ryan never saw eye to eye. Never. We come from different backgrounds, different perspectives." Although born in Castlepollard, Co. Westmeath, Gogarty grew up in the Palmerstown and Lucan areas of Dublin. He went to school in Lucan, before studying for a diploma in journalism in Rathmines' College of Commerce and finding work as a journalist and editor. Ryan's path was somewhat different, moving from national school in Dundrum to Gonzaga College in Ranelagh and on to University College Dublin (UCD). Gogarty railed against what he called the "southside wing of the party", which appeared to include pretty much everyone expect himself and, presumably, Boyle and White. According to Gormley, even Sargent, who represented Dublin North, "originally came from a leafy southside suburb and then relocated up to Balbriggan."

Gogarty said he was keen to balance his critical remarks about Ryan by describing the former Minister as a nice guy and a family man, and by stressing that he was the right person to lead the party in the aftermath of the 2011 General Election. "Eamon's got a lot of strengths. He's always really positive, he always focuses on the visionary ... I think he's the best person to be leader at the moment. He has the time, he has the income and he's also media friendly. He's a good communicator. I've nothing against him, but I was annoyed over the presidency."

Gogarty's grudge stemmed from September 2004, when Ryan embarked on something of a solo run and gave the impression that not only would the Greens have a candidate in the presidential election, but also that that candidate would be him. Gogarty said Ryan had called into his office unexpectedly one Monday morning: "And he said, 'Listen there's going to be something about the presidency and me coming up in the media.' And I said, 'Right, is that coming from you or is that coming from the media?' And he said, 'A bit of both.'" Gogarty said he told Ryan there and then he did not think the party should field a candidate and that he would oppose such a proposition at every stage. Ryan appeared on RTÉ Radio One's News at One programme later that day giving the impression that his candidacy was a done deal. "That made my blood totally boil," Gogarty said.

Trevor Sargent and Gormley were also none too keen on the idea of getting involved in a presidential election. Gogarty was furious because Ryan had not formally sought his colleagues' endorsement, and he told the reporter Charlie Bird so. Bird broadcast the story on the evening news, naturally, and at the next meeting of the Green parliamentary party, Gogarty claimed to have given Ryan "the mother of all bollockings" in front of colleagues. "I just said it's a disgrace; how dare you. I really, really ate him." Although Ryan's natural tendency was to avoid conflict if at all possible, he surely must have been tempted to get his revenge on Gogarty in the aftermath of his thuggish outburst against Stagg in 2009. But, despite the private pasting Gogarty had given him in 2004, he resisted, something Gogarty gives him credit for: "In fairness, I didn't get anything like that after the Emmet Stagg thing … maybe I did deserve it then."

However, the Green parliamentarians were put in a position where they simply had to publicly endorse Ryan in order to avoid embarrassment for the party and humiliation for the potential candidate. "Myself and John Gormley think along the same lines and one of the things was we have to endorse Eamon Ryan … because obviously that would've been humiliating for him if we didn't – and the Greens would've looked pretty stupid – so we endorsed him anyway." Sargent, meanwhile, was also pretty angry with Gogarty for blurting out the party's problem to Charlie Bird and ruining the carefully constructed appearance of unity the Greens so liked to present.

By this stage, many youngsters could not recall the last time Ireland had had a man in the role of president of the country, such was the success of Mary McAleese and her talented predecessor Mary Robinson. Launching her bid for another seven-year term, the incumbent was asked how she would feel about the prospect of a man (Ryan) entering the race. With a smile, McAleese simply said she believed men added spice to life. Meanwhile, the fretting Green TDs and Senators headed to Clonakilty in Co. Cork where the party's National Executive Council (NEC) was meeting. There they were astonished to find buoyant delegates delighted with the media attention Ryan's proposed bid had engendered. The Green Clare county councillor Brian Meaney summed up a widespread view among the Green grassroots when he proclaimed: "We have had more exposure in the last two days than we have had for 20 years." Gogarty understood the party members' feelings – he too clearly craved media attention, after all – although he disagreed strongly with their thinking. "The membership loved it because we were being talked about in a positive light rather than a bunch of hippies. I felt like the wicked witch at the christening," he said. He was concerned that the grassroots were beginning to look at Ryan as a "messiah." The Dublin Mid-West deputy was, yet again, "pretty peeved" and ready to resign "in outrage" if the membership had endorsed Ryan, although very much aware that he was coming across like "the whiner at the wedding."

In the event, Ryan stepped back from the precipice despite his previously expressed ambition. He advised delegates he would not seek to contest the presidential election, citing difficulties in securing a nomination as the reason for his withdrawal. "That deflated a lot of balloons", Gogarty admitted. Knowing that potential presidential nominees needed the support of 20 members of the Oireachtas or four county councils, Ryan had crunched the numbers and come to a painfully realistic conclusion. The Greens had six TDs, and a handful of Independents would have supported Ryan: Shane Ross, now an Independent TD for Dublin South but then a Senator; Independent TD for Dublin North

Central Finian McGrath and the late Dublin Central deputy Tony Gregory. Additional backers would probably have come from within the Labour Party, especially after then leader Pat Rabbitte described Ryan in extremely flattering terms as the most intelligent new TD elected in 2002. The Labour Party had failed to have any new candidates returned that year, obviously. There was a significant rump within Labour opposed to backing Ryan however, and it would have created an awkward situation for both parties, particularly as Michael D. Higgins was clearly annoyed by his colleagues' lack of support for his intense desire to contest that year. A reality check in the form of a briefing on the extremely expensive cost of a presidential campaign, not presented by Ryan who did not concern himself with such materialistic matters, appeared to have influenced delegates strongly during the course of the five-hour meeting. After all, the Greens remained members of a small party without wealthy backers who had tended to run campaigns on a shoestring. The apparently unbeatable McAleese was subsequently returned unopposed to the Áras for a second term.

The saga set Ryan apart from the common or garden variety of Green. He had been an anonymous enough deputy, not widely known outside his Dublin South constituency, who had suddenly gained a national profile and an invaluable appearance on the Marian Finucane radio programme, during which he acknowledged that he had used cannabis in the past – a revelation that was barely greeted with a shoulder shrug by the Green grassroots. The entire episode did Ryan no harm, however, and probably quite a bit of good. "It does say a lot about a person," Gogarty said. "Some people call it ego some people would call it vision. Why would anyone put their name forward as president, right? Eamon Ryan obviously believes this is good for the Green Party ... And it is good for Eamon Ryan: he's the party leader now, obviously it put him into an echelon ... It put him into a different league. Eamon Ryan has the vision. If you look at all the media commentary at the time: Eamon Ryan: brave, audacious, outside the box." Ryan would go on to tell the *Sunday Business Post* political correspondent Niamh Connolly in August 2011 that "looking back, it would have been the right thing" for the Greens to have run a candidate in 2004.

Surprisingly, White described Ryan as "quite a shy man behind it all." She added: "I don't know Eamon very well even now, not really ... I can't say I know him terribly well. The others I can read more easily." Ryan could come across as whiter than white, and indeed the moral anguish he experienced when Shell to Sea campaigner Maura Harrington went on hunger strike over Shell's plan to lay the Corrib offshore gas pipeline sent him scurrying to the confessional box. But there would be more testing crises for the Minister to come, which would see him so stressed out he would revert to that most unGreen habit of smoking.

Inter- and intra-party rivalries were put aside at the tail end of 2009 when it emerged that the Minister for Finance Brian

Lenihan, then a 50-year-old father of two teenagers, had been diagnosed with pancreatic cancer shortly before Christmas. The news shocked the country, but early in the New Year Lenihan was back to work. He announced it was his intention to continue to serve as Minister for Finance, having discussed the matter with the Taoiseach and consulted his medical advisers, and his bravery in the face of adversity was admired by all.

CHAPTER 7

THE TWEET THAT BROUGHT DOWN A GOVERNMENT MINISTER

THE GREEN PARTY'S PARLIAMENTARIANS OFTEN SEEMED TO BE speaking a completely different language from that of their coalition counterparts, and this was particularly the case when the junior partners used new technology to communicate. The Greens prided themselves on keeping up to speed with all the latest gadgets and means of electronic communication. John Gormley boasted of being the first elected representative in Ireland to have an email address, and he was certainly one of the earliest to be seen sporting an iPad around the Leinster House canteen at a time when many other deputies had never even heard of a smartphone.

Trevor Sargent's often unintentionally hilarious organic food-growing blog, "Trevor's Kitchen Garden", seemed to prove an endlessly fruitful resource for colour writers. Ciaran Cuffe, probably the most technically advanced politician of his generation, explained the concept of blogging to uninitiated *Irish Times* readers way back in 2006 in an article he penned about the most up-to-date trends in modern political communications.

"In the blogosphere, people expect less formality and more

emotion. It's a *tu* rather than *vous* world," Cuffe said. Dan Boyle certainly provided the emotion once he mastered the art of Twitter, and effectively brought down a Fianna Fáil Minister with a timely tweet in February 2010.

Boyle had stumbled across Twitter a year earlier, setting up an account on 21 February 2009, which was relatively late in the lifespan of the micro-blogging website. While he was canvassing ahead of the European elections, a close female friend suggested some new methods he might consider experimenting with in his ongoing attempts to find new ways to communicate with potential voters, although she was sceptical about the value of Twitter.

"When I was running in the European elections a good friend of mine encouraged me to go on Facebook and talked about Twitter as well. She wasn't that supportive of Twitter, I must admit, but I kind of discovered Twitter then." He barely used the platform at all for a few months but then embraced it with gusto and was thrilled when his number of followers began to climb up and up. Other Greens were busy stamping their logo on gardening gloves or organising creative photocalls in order to get the attention of voters, but Boyle chose to stay online.

Boyle was well ahead of the pack when it came to communicating directly and interacting with members of the public at a time when most elected representatives preferred to use the filter of a spokesperson, but being so accessible to politically-savvy punters certainly had its downsides. Sometimes the tone of the Twitter conversations was constructive, but often it was hostile and bitterly confrontational. Boyle's unmatched ability to rub people up the wrong way tended to come to the fore when he used this particular medium. He either was not interested or did not know how to diffuse an argument, and he ended up feeling he had to block a number of followers when their comments became incessantly critical. "And then the Willie O'Dea thing happened, which wasn't premeditated as such," he said.

The "Willie O'Dea thing", as Boyle dubbed it, was a rather bizarre story that had been rumbling under the surface of mainstream media discourse for some time. The tale had its origins in January 2009, when three Brazilian women suspected of running a brothel in Limerick were arrested following a raid on a Clancy Strand apartment by gardai. The owner of the apartment, who had not known what it was being used for, happened to be Nessan Quinlivan. He had been an IRA escapee from Brixton Prison in the early 1990s. Quinlivan's younger brother Maurice was a Sinn Féin candidate in the upcoming local elections. The younger Quinlivan had been critical of O'Dea, then Fianna Fáil's Minister for Defence, highlighting the fact that Department of Defence headed notepaper had been used to write letters to planning applicants. He also claimed high costs were associated with civil servants employed to help O'Dea with constituency affairs. On 9 March, at the launch of Fianna Fáil's local election campaign in the town, Limerick Leader reporter Mike Dwane conducted a brief interview with O'Dea in which the Minister responded robustly to the criticism from the Sinn Féin camp. "They are running a big campaign. The money from the Northern Bank must be stretching fairly far. Quote me on that," O'Dea told Dwane.

"While occasionally we send out letters to planning applicants on the wrong paper, we have never been involved with anyone who shot anybody, or robbed banks, or kidnapped people."

Dwane was using a digital dictaphone to record the Minister's comments, which he held close to O'Dea's famous moustache. There was no question therefore of O'Dea being unaware he was being taped, but this did not tempter the robust nature of his remarks.

"I suppose I'm going a bit too far when I say this but I'd like to ask Mr Quinlivan is the brothel still closed?" O'Dea continued. Dwane was nonplussed, having recently returned from holidays and knowing nothing about the brothel story. "What brothel is that Willie?" he asked. O'Dea replied: "Do you know the brothel they found in his name and in his brother's name down in Clancy Strand?" Dwane said he had not heard anything about such a development.

"Did you not hear that? You better check with your sources. There was a house owned by him that was rented out and they found two ladies of the night operating there in the last couple of weeks."

Naturally, Dwane contacted Maurice Quinlivan seeking a response to O'Dea's false claims. Quinlivan issued proceedings against O'Dea after Dwane's story appeared in print, quoting

O'Dea asking Quinlivan if the brothel had closed. He also sought an injunction to prevent O'Dea from repeating the ownership allegation. O'Dea swore an affidavit in which he denied having told the reporter that Quinlivan part-owned the apartment. When Dwane read the affidavit he immediately realised it did not tally with the interview he had conducted, which O'Dea himself acknowledged when he read the transcript. O'Dea's lawyers then contacted Quinlivan's legal team to say his recollection of the interview had been incorrect and that he had in fact stated to Dwane that Quinlivan had an involvement with the premises in question, but that remark had subsequently escaped his memory. Accepting that he had defamed Quinlivan, who had by this stage been elected as a councillor, O'Dea paid him damages and costs.

The matter was briefly reported in the national press in December but not until Fine Gael Senator Eugene Regan accused O'Dea of perjury in the Seanad the following February did the controversy spark up again. With O'Dea facing mounting pressure to explain the extremely confusing situation, Eamon Ryan passed the Government chief whip Pat Carey on the Ministerial corridor. Carey's hangdog expression was even more pronounced than usual. Nodding at Ryan, he rolled his doleful eyes and muttered "God help us".

Fine Gael leader Enda Kenny notified the Dáil of his intention to introduce a motion of no confidence in the Minister on 17 February, 2010. Naturally enough, the Greens, as Fianna

Fáil's partners in Government, were expected to contribute to the ensuing debate. A breakdown in communications meant that some of the Greens appeared only to become aware of the scheduling of the motion a few hours before it was debated. Ryan was hastily selected to speak for the Greens and put in what can best be described as a sheepish and unenthusiastic performance. As Ryan remembered it, he was in the middle of a meeting when there was a knock at the door asking him to scramble for the Dáil chamber to speak on the motion.

"You're running a Department flat out; you're trying to keep up to speed with an economic crisis and trying to keep in touch with other people so you understand what's happening there; you've got political stuff going on in your own party, and I was aware just from reading the papers about this issue down in Limerick," he said. "Knock at the door, 'Quick there's a vote of confidence in the Dáil. We have to speak; we have to put someone forward to speak. Will you do it?'" Ryan agreed, reluctantly, to speak on behalf of the party and called into Gormley's office "literally on the way" to the chamber. Gormley had been talking to O'Dea, "and Willie had said to him, 'Don't worry it'll all be cleared up tomorrow in the Limerick Leader.'" In the course of the rushed conversation, Ryan said he asked Gormley: "What do I say? What do I do? How do we play it?" There was not enough time to formulate a sophisticated strategy, so they simply agreed that Ryan should "just not whip it up further."

And so a mortified Ryan embarked upon one of the worst

performances of his life, stuttering and acting like a man with a bad smell under his nose and peppering his reluctant contribution with qualifications as he backed O'Dea on what he said was turning out to be a "frantic" day for the Greens. "Politically for me it was dynamite, it was desperate stuff. You should never do it because you just go out and you're batting for something that you can't easily defend. You don't have the full facts at your disposal," he said. "So I tried to be as kind of vague or as kind of noncommittal one way or the other, but at the same time I didn't want the Government to fall [over this]," he added. "So I went in and gave the speech which was hugely damaging to me personally, but I did it on the basis that I don't want the Government to fall on this issue which I don't even know – no one knows – the full details of." Meanwhile, Boyle was sitting in his office watching Ryan's contribution in the Dáil chamber on a monitor with a growing sense of despair.

"Well I felt sorry for him. I did, because at that stage, that was early in the debate, I could see what he was trying to do. He was trying to be supportive, but not. I mean, it was so full of non sequiturs and qualifications. But that didn't make me angry; that made me sad." Boyle's anger was directed elsewhere. "I was furious with a few people: our programme manager, the parliamentary party and the fact that a decision was made without us meeting as a group." The rowdy and at times jocular contributions from O'Dea and some other Fianna Fáil figures infuriated Boyle even more.

O'Dea's defence was that he had made a mistake, which he had already acknowledged and apologised for. He also took a few swipes at Fine Gael, Labour and Sinn Féin in the course of his mud-slinging contribution to the debate in the Dáil. O'Dea had asked the then Minister for Justice Dermot Ahern to go into the chamber and speak on his behalf. Ahern took the difficult decision to say no to a party and Ministerial colleague, explaining that he was declining on the grounds that he was Minister for Justice and the matter was about an affidavit. But thinking that if he ever happened to find himself in trouble in future he would certainly like someone to stand by him in his hour of need, Ahern sat beside O'Dea in the chamber. While he did not make a formal address, he heckled the Opposition robustly. Boyle despaired. "I thought they were utterly appalling. They weren't addressing the issue, they were just engaging in the same name-calling that passes for debate," he sighed. He recalled being made very aware of a large amount of what he described as "dissention" from Green Party members outside Leinster House, many of whom were phoning his Seanad office or his mobile phone to express their displeasure with the approach the leadership had adopted and were asking what exactly he planned to do about the matter. He continued to watch the Dáil proceedings as O'Dea survived the motion of no confidence, thanks to the support of the Greens. To cap it all, some Fianna Fáil TDs literally administered friendly pats on the back to a few Green colleagues in the chamber in the immediate aftermath the vote. The optics of the situation were a disaster for the Greens. All in all, it was a damaging day for the junior coalition partner, which had always prided itself on its commitment to standards in public office.

Boyle's tweeting finger hovered over the 'new tweet' icon on his iPhone. "It was more or less Willie O'Dea's own performance. And leaving aside the fact of whether it was perjury or not, what it represents in terms of politics I still find appalling: that you engage in a debate with a political opponent by talking about brothels. It's seedy and all the rest of it and I wanted nothing to do with it, so that's why I tweeted," Boyle explained. So, in well under the maximum of 140 characters allowed by the concise medium, Boyle complained that he was "not happy" with what had happened and expressed a belief that the Greens had been "bounced" into supporting the motion, although Carey would subsequently insist he was not aware of any Green objection to tabling the motion of confidence on the Wednesday. For good measure, Boyle tweeted again: "As regards to Minister O'Dea I don't have confidence in him. His situation is compromised. Probably be a few chapters in this story yet." There certainly would be.

Boyle firmly believed that the senior Green Ministers had been influenced by the benefits attached to the quite positive relationship they enjoyed with O'Dea at the Cabinet table. O'Dea had pleasantly surprised Gormley and Ryan by emerging as "a perceived ally within the Cabinet" because "he seemed to be more reasonable than others", Boyle said. "John and Eamon got on well with Willie … I think they wanted the vote of confidence to pass over quickly. That's why the initial unhappiness was: that there was a lack of understanding about how badly it was playing within the party." Ryan recalled Boyle's obvious distress that evening. "Dan was very unhappy, rightly. Politically it was just one of those ones where you couldn't support. It was just everything that we were not in politics for, that type of politics." Boyle's expression of his disquiet through tweeting had "a fairly strong effect", Ryan remembered. But in reality the immediate feedback from the Green parliamentary party about his rogue comments was "largely negative", Boyle said. Cuffe, Mary White and Paul Gogarty were particularly angry, with Gormley and Ryan less obviously unhappy. "Paul felt I'd undermined the parliamentary party and the actions they'd already taken, but subsequently I think everyone did approve of it," Boyle said. "Eamon would freely admit it was the right thing to do subsequently."

The following morning, a "flash PP" was called. This had become the Green shorthand term for a sudden or "flash" parliamentary party meeting, more often than not called in an emergency situation, when TDs and Senators would receive an urgent text message, stop whatever they happened to be doing at the time and rush towards a large corner room on the third floor of Agriculture House, an architectural monstrosity on Kildare Street. "That was one of the logistical challenges to get us all together and up in that room, which was several minutes walk away from the kind of centre of gravity of the Dáil," Cuffe recalled. The entire parliamentary party attended except for Sargent who was in Nuremberg at an organic food event. On the table in the centre of the room were numerous copies of the latest edition of the *Limerick Leader* newspaper, procured from the shop around the corner that stocked regional papers from all over Ireland. The Leader was read over by the Green TDs and Senators, because O'Dea had assured Gormley that an upcoming article would vindicate him, but that did not happen as far as the Greens were concerned. The reality of the situation was that Boyle's tweet had put the Greens in a corner. The facts before them had not changed, but the political necessity was finally dawning and so they reversed their decision of the previous night and began to say O'Dea could not now continue as a member of Government.

The Green TDs left the meeting at one point for a Dáil vote, but the full team resumed after lunch, by which time O'Dea had taken part in a live interview with Sean O'Rourke on the News at One programme on RTÉ Radio One. The presenter had opened the fraught exchange with a killer line directed towards the beleaguered Minister: "You really are a one hell of a dirty fighter, aren't you?" When extracts of Dwane's tape were dramatically broadcast during the lunchtime programme, O'Dea's "You better check with your sources" line sounded even worse and ten times sneakier than it looked in print. The interview proved extremely damaging for O'Dea. Fianna Fáil sources said O'Dea and Brian Cowen had a telephone conversation immediately after the broadcast, during which it was decided O'Dea would resign. However, Green sources insisted a decision was not taken until the time Gormley went to meet Cowen shortly after 3 pm. "John went to Brian Cowen, set out the approach and … pretty much it led to the resignation of Willy," Ryan said.

O'Dea's resignation was finally announced on the night of 18 February. There were further twists in the tale, however. On 19 February, O'Dea controversially contradicted the Taoiseach's account of his resignation and backed Gormley's version of the events that had led to his departure from office. Cowen had said O'Dea had come to the conclusion he must resign from Cabinet without any coercion from him or the Green Party, but Gormley maintained that he had told the Taoiseach in no uncertain terms that O'Dea's position was untenable and the stability of the Government would be under threat if he remained on in office. O'Dea's downfall reflected well on the Greens, as it briefly countered the perception that the party had a cosy relationship with Fianna Fáil. O'Dea's attitude towards the Greens was "quite negative afterwards, that's for sure," Boyle said. But O'Dea would get the last laugh when he was returned to the Dáil to represent Limerick City in 2011, having been told by the DPP he had no case to answer, while all the Greens lost their seats.

It is not an exaggeration to say that Boyle's tweet about O'Dea changed political communications. He had actually put his comment up on old-fashioned Facebook first, but it went largely unnoticed thanks to the interest in the newer social networking website. "It started getting picked up … and that's how the myth and legend was produced," Boyle said. It also changed the way he addressed the media. "I rarely ever issued a press release after that because that became the means of communication. Most of the things I was quoted on was either what I said in the Seanad or what I tweeted," he said. His online pronouncements also did something to change the way journalists worked in Leinster House. Those still in possession of old-fashioned mobile phones that could only deal with calls and texts, or who did not yet have a Twitter account, began to feel left behind, while the particularly advanced set up new accounts to monitor the output of politicians exclusively. Online reporters, in particular, began scouring Twitter feeds for the latest nugget of news. For a short while, the medium risked becoming more important than the message. Twitter did not respect traditional media deadlines and reporters would be harassed by their editors at all hours, alerting them to the latest political tweet, however mundane.

The verbose Boyle admitted the enforced brevity of the format, allowing complex views to be expressed only in 140 letters or symbols, created some problems for him. "It causes a lot of trouble, but it's a sound bite culture so that's where the skill comes in. And I'm still trying to master it, I must admit." But he rejected accusations of hyperactivity. "I haven't tweeted as much as people think I have ... it's about four or five a day or something like that," he said. Among the political correspondents in Leinster House, Boyle came to be seen as an outrider who was free to express the views of the party's TDs, although this was not always the case and he created many headaches for the party's communications team as a result. "I had this out with John Downing a lot of times ... John, as the press adviser to the party, came up with this line of 'That's Dan Boyle speaking in a personal capacity,'" Boyle chuckled. His relentless tweeting also created a problem for Gormley in the aftermath of the O'Dea saga. "John got into trouble because either he intimated or he intimated subsequently that he liked the fact that I tweeted and it was a useful way of expressing our unhappiness about issues, and that suddenly got legs and some people thought there was some sort of co-ordination between myself and John." There was not, Boyle insisted. "No not at all. He's not the boss of me."

If Green colleagues were sometimes left bewildered by Boyle's machinations on Twitter, emotions within Fianna Fáil ranged from bemusement to fury. In May 2010, a senior backbencher known to be close to Cowen issued a stern warning to Boyle to stop his "irresponsible" tweets. The message from Limerick West TD John Cregan was widely interpreted as having come directly from the mouth of Cowen. Cregan described Boyle's postings as "frustrating" and recommended the Senator work through any problems with Government policy within the confines of his parliamentary party. Fianna Fáil backbenchers were doing their best to maintain good relations with the Coalition partners, Cregan claimed. But a defiant Boyle refused to compromise and made clear he had no intention of giving up his beloved twitter account. "I'm not in Fianna Fáil: different style, different party, different culture. I prefer to engage with people rather than do things behind closed doors," he said. The Greens often complained that the electorate judged their party by a higher moral standard than was applied to Fianna Fáil. But the Greens themselves encouraged this with their generally sniffy attitude about Fianna Fáil's standards in office.

There was further trauma ahead for the Greens the following week, and this time trouble would strike much closer to home. Sargent resigned his Ministry after admitting to contacting a garda about a case involving a constituent. The entire political establishment was surprised that Sargent, of all people, would become embroiled in such a controversy. One woman TD from another party, shaking her head in disbelief, said: "He's as dull as dishwater, but just so decent." For the Greens, this latest revelation was no laughing matter. Sargent's resignation, and the speed at which it happened, shook the party to its core.

Ryan recalled that Tuesday in late February as a "very dramatic day", with momentous events that would normally be played out over a series of weeks or months telescoped into just 24 hours: "It literally happened in one day." The story had appeared in the morning version of the *Evening Herald* newspaper, and the Green parliamentarians' mobiles came alive with texts and phone calls heralding yet another "flash PP" in Agriculture House. A victim of an assault, who was a constituent of Sargent's in Dublin North but had no connection with the Green Party, had outlined frustration at the slow progress of a legal case to the TD in 2008. The constituent had remonstrated with local children who were trying to remove a road sign in their housing estate. He then became involved in a dispute over the matter with the father of a local child. Both men were convicted of threatening and abusive behaviour and were fined €500 in relation to the incident, and the child's father receiving further sanction for assault which he appealed. The constituent had contacted Sargent, who wrote a letter to the garda investigating the case expressing shock that the man had ended up being charged with an offence. In an inappropriate intervention, he wrote: "It is, I believe, wholly inappropriate to proceed with this summons at this point."

Seeking to influence a case had left Sargent's position compromised, and he and his party colleagues knew it. All were wondering how the man who was considered the party's moral compass could have got it so wrong? "You're kind of aware of it in the morning; you get a phone call at 11 o'clock: quickly come to a meeting," Ryan remembered. "So you're there in your Department or whatever and it's 'down tools' ... And so then you kind of get together and look at the letter and you kind of go, 'Hmmm.'" There was none of the long-drawn out moral wrangling that had characterised other recent meetings, however; Sargent did not dither. "Without anything being said Trevor said, 'Look I see it. It was a mistake. I'm going to resign.'" Nobody tried to stop the former leader. "No, not to my recall," said Ryan, "it was his call; it was his decision." Events moved quickly after that. "So you see yourself half an hour later walking into the Dáil behind him as he's about to resign." Sargent briefly told the Dáil he accepted he had made an error of judgment and would tender his resignation as Minister of State for Food and Horticulture.

Almost immediately, there were claims that leaks about the letter had come from Fianna Fáil sources, with some senior Opposition deputies happy to stoke up the levels of paranoia that already existed in the by now unstable Government. They argued that the timing could not be purely coincidental, coming so soon after O'Dea's resignation. Labour's Pat Rabbitte humorously suggested it was a case of "the empire strikes back." A swarm of photographers were cordoned-off at the bottom of the Leinster House plinth, where they waited impatiently for a fresh snap of Sargent. Eventually the Green TDs and Senators emerged from Leinster House: Boyle sheltering the slight figure of Sargent with an umbrella while rain pelted his light grey suit.

The bewildered Greens then huddled together seeking shelter in the portico outside LH2000 that dark evening. It was clear they were now unsure who they could trust. An unusually candid, and visibly shaken, Gormley admitted to being in an "emotional state" and "shell-shocked." Gormley was asked if he rejected the accusation put forward by some Opposition spokespeople that Fianna Fáil had leaked the information that had resulted in Sargent's resignation. Ominously for the Coalition's stability, he would only say he did not have possession of all the facts and the Opposition might want to use the situation to undermine the Government. There was no clear expression of trust in Fianna Fáil.

Instead, Gormley said he wanted to focus on paying tribute to a man who was his friend, adding that Sargent had resigned in an honourable and decent way. Looking drawn, he rested a protective hand on Sargent's shoulder. Even the ever-upbeat Ryan admitted that "the Trevor thing was difficult."

Sargent's nerves were clearly much steadier than those of his colleagues. He was in chatty form and looked cool and collected. Astonishingly, while he said he regretted what he had done, he robustly defended the motivation behind his action. He said people all around the country could relate to the kind of situation he had encountered in his constituency because the scourge of anti-social behaviour affected everyone. He did not want to see people refraining from being good citizens. "I think we should not be sending out a message to people that if you are afraid of intimidation you should therefore ignore law-breaking. That's the wrong message to send to people," he said. "That was the only motivation I had, was to be of support to a constituent in their time of need." There was only one explanation for it: Sargent was in early election mode. He promptly donated his Ministerial severance pay to charity. Although his colleagues clearly respected him as much as ever, there was a sense that Sargent pulled away from the parliamentary party somewhat in the aftermath of the incident. Boyle said: "Trevor, especially when he resigned … became concerned about retaining his seat, so while he participated in parliamentary party meetings his focus was as much on Dublin North as much as anything else at that stage I think."

Chapter 8

Gormley gets a 'Dear John' letter

There were other high-profile resignations creating political sensations around this time, of course. George Lee, who had left RTÉ to sweep to victory in the Dublin South byelection as a so-called 'celebrity' candidate, stormed out of Fine Gael and dramatically departed the Dáil after just nine months on 8 February 2010. He complained he had "virtually no influence or input" in shaping Fine Gael's economic policies during a period of enormous economic upheaval. Lee had taken an unpaid leave of absence from the national broadcaster, which was due to end in May, and he returned to RTÉ although not as economics editor.

The Greens, like all participants in and observers of Irish politics, looked on in amazement as Fine Gael was convulsed by the astonishing development. But disgruntlement had been brewing within the Greens' own ranks, as a 'Dear John' letter from one of their Senators to the party leader was soon to prove. The resignation of Senator Deirdre de Burca received a fraction of the amount of attention outside the Leinster House bubble as Lee's spectacular departure from politics just four days earlier, but it rattled the party badly. The remaining Green parliamentarians closed ranks as de Burca fulminated publicly against the party. She distributed the contents of her resignation letter to eager media outlets. "Dear John," it began, "I am writing to inform you of my intention to resign from the Green Party Parliamentary Party and from Seanad Éireann with immediate effect."

De Burca did not hold back. She accused the party of having gradually abandoned its political values and integrity and, woundingly, said it had evolved into "no more than an extension of the Fianna Fáil party." The disastrous local and European elections in June of the previous year seemed to have left the party "paralysed," she said. "Any suggestion that we challenge Fianna Fáil, or face it down over important issues, seems to bring up a great fear in us that we will have to leave Government." She claimed that staying in Government appeared to have become an end in itself for the Green Party. "While I was always aware that our political inexperience as a party would leave us vulnerable to being manipulated by Fianna Fáil in government, what I hadn't predicted was the strong attachment to office that appears to have developed since we became part of Government."

De Burca also revealed confidential goings-on at daily party meetings, at which discussions routinely centred on the problems Greens faced in getting Fianna Fáil to co-operate with the actual implementation of policy the junior partner had worked so hard to get the senior party to agree to. De Burca came across as someone who had been grudgingly impressed by Fianna Fáil's skill: "From stonewalling us and trying to unravel key aspects of our policy initiatives being implemented, to ignoring our input into the preparation of new legislation, to reneging on two key agreements made between Party Leaders, the Fianna Fáil Party continues to 'run rings' around us and to take advantage of our inexperience and our very obvious fear of facing the electorate."

De Burca claimed Gormley had been asked on many occasions to adopt a tougher stance in his approach to Brian Cowen, but he had "clearly been unable, or unwilling to do so." The result of this weakness had been a haemorrhaging of support from the party, she said.

De Burca's case was somewhat undermined by the fact that her fury at not getting a particular job in Brussels had triggered her resignation, which raised the question: Would she have kept her concerns about the direction the Greens were going in to herself if she had succeeded in getting the post she wanted? The new EU Commissioner was former Fianna Fáil minister Maire Geoghegan-Quinn. De Burca claimed the Greens had lobbied for former European Parliament president Pat Cox to get the position – although Cox said this was news to him – but supported Geoghegan-Quinn on the condition that a Green would be appointed to her cabinet.

Gormley subsequently told de Burca she had been "shafted" by Fianna Fáil when it turned out that all positions in the cabinet had been filled, she claimed. While a defection never looks good in politics, the Greens were saying privately that they were happy enough to see the back of de Burca. One aide, speaking only half in jest, said: "Thank God. Now we've got rid of all the mad, curly-haired women." Mary White took her to task publicly in a letter to party members, accusing her of having levelled "scathing, unfair and totally groundless criticisms" against Gormley.

Mark Dearey was quickly drafted in to replace de Burca. The "businessman, vintner, and music promoter", as the Government statement announcing his appointment described him, was sitting in the Seanad chamber with his colleagues Dan Boyle and Niall Ó Brolcháin within a fortnight. The newcomer owned the popular pub and music venue, The Spirit Store, in Dundalk and became a member of Dundalk Town Council in 2004 and Louth County Council in 2009. While some considered the likeable Dearey too nice for politics, he was rated highly by Gormley and showed he did not lack ambition when he ran for the deputy leader's position after the 2011 General Election.

Reflecting on that hectic period, Ryan said he regretted the way the whole thing was handled. "The Deirdre thing was difficult," he said. While the party played it down at the time, the episode was extremely uncomfortable for the tight-knit Greens. "Deirdre left because Maire Geoghegan-Quinn appointed a cabinet and Deirdre hadn't got a post in it ... I just think in hindsight that whole process was a very regrettable one and one that we should have handled and done differently," Ryan said. "George Lee had similarly resigned. It was just one of those times when one thing triggers off another, and it was a 'rat-tat-tat-tat' of kind of political changes that did not reflect well on the general political system." The cumulative effect of the resignations of Willie O'Dea, Trevor Sargent, Lee and de Burca in such quick succession was to damage the body politic. "None of the instances were something that would reassure the public to say, 'Oh, here's a political system that knows exactly what its doing; has got it act together'. Actually I think the biggest difficulty was in the loss of public confidence. With each of the issues you could think, OK there are merits one way or the other, but the accumulation of those four things at the time when the country needed to get back its confidence, needed to lift its spirits and confidence in the political system, they did a lot of damage."

The atmosphere in the Dáil chamber had by this stage become poisonous. In March, the Labour leader Eamon Gilmore managed to provoke a passionate response from the increasingly introverted Brian Cowen by striking a nerve when he accused the Taoiseach of "economic treason." The sleeping giant appeared to wake from his slumber at the words. "I will not be accused of seeking to commit treason against my country. I consider that to be beyond the Pale," Cowen fumed. "He took personal umbrage," Ryan recalled. Public confidence in the Government was further damaged by Cowen's frequently poor Dáil performances, Ryan said.

"In that period the public was watching on the six o'clock news, the nine o'clock news, and they were seeing the debate in the Dáil and they were increasingly saying, 'I don't like what's going on, or I don't trust, or I don't know what's going on,'" he said. This was particularly the case given that radio and television programmes were by now finding it practically impossible to persuade Fianna Fáil guests to appear on their shows. A Fianna Fáil boycott of broadcaster Pat Kenny's Frontline programme on RTÉ 1 would soon be proposed at a meeting of the parliamentary party, with Limerick West TD Niall Collins saying Fianna Fáil guests were treated merely as "the entertainment" and baited by audience members. Ryan continued: "The Dáil is actually very important. If you're not going to go on TV and do [Tonight With] Vincent Browne [on TV3], where you are out is in the Dáil and you have to win in the Dáil. You have to win in Leaders Questions, you have to win in key speeches and so on in the Dáil. And I think Eamon Gilmore in particular, and to a lesser extent Enda Kenny, they won in the Dáil. They won in those kind of key ten-second sound bites on the nine o'clock news. They were winning that battle." Meanwhile, Ryan said, an apparently endless round of celebrity economists and other experts where appearing on the media saying the Government's economic policy was not the appropriate one to have adopted or continued to follow. "It's no surprise that the confidence in the political approach starts to wane and that's the problem," he said. Also in March, a Green representative on Wicklow Town Council, Pat Kavanagh, resigned from the party saying she felt let down. The Green Party was no longer the party she signed up to and it no longer represented her position. She could not stand over decisions made at Government level, particularly those relating to Nama.

Talks on a Cabinet reshuffle got underway between Cowen and Gormley around this time. The Green leader was under pressure from his own people to secure an extra junior Minister, while Cowen was facing calls from within the Fianna Fáil camp not to concede an inch to the Greens. The junior Coalition party pointed to the agreement struck with Bertie Ahern in 2007 which they believed committed Cowen to allowing the Greens an extra Minister of State half way through the life of the Coalition, although no-one with an ounce of political nous actually believed the shaky Coalition would now run its full term. Paul Gogarty claimed Cowen was stonewalling. "It became apparent that Cowen was basically suggesting he knew nothing about this arrangement: 'I know nothing about this with Bertie; I don't know what youse are on about lads,'" Gogarty said. Cowen's statement irritated the Greens, Gogarty said, although – given previous experience of Ahern – "it might have been true." He added: "It was a gentleman's agreement with Bertie, stupidly." The Greens had been heavily involved in seeking a reduction in the number of junior ministers from 20 to 15 the previous year, which was granted, so some Fianna Fáil deputies claimed any deal struck with Ahern was null and void as a result.

Meanwhile, word had leaked out that the Greens had a bizarre plan to rotate Gormley's Cabinet post at the half-way point of the Government, to allow Ciaran Cuffe to take over as Minister for the Environment. The most unusual idea smacked of an innocence the Greens might have possessed before they were blooded in

Government, and was described as "very messy politically" by Ryan. "We had what you might call a naive understanding or too clever by half, whichever, but in going into Government, in the sense that [being] a party that's not obsessed by power, that we would have an arrangement half way through where we would reshuffle ministries." The idea of the party leader leaving his Cabinet position halfway through the Government's term seemed ridiculous, particularly when the economy was in such a sorry state. The principle of rotation, from a Green perspective, meant "you don't get tied into your position: you're there to serve, so you rotate", according to Paul Gogarty. The belief was that "everyone who might have egos or conflicting ideas about how great they are, everyone got a slice of the opportunity." Another function of the arrangement would be that it would protect the leader's position from potential challengers, Gogarty argued. "Trevor probably felt you've got different ambitious people in the parliamentary party and as well as the principled idea of rotation this might make sure that no-one's going to be jockeying for position."

Whatever the motivation behind the plan originally, Ryan conceded the idea as originally conceived was not a wise one. "That in hindsight was not a clever idea," he admitted. And it most certainly did not go down well with the public who were becoming increasingly disenchanted with the Green's preoccupations as the economic crisis continued to bite. "I think that was particularly the case when people learned, hang on, they've got some internal arrangements that they'll change ministries. That just went down like an absolute lead balloon with the Irish public, and I think understandably so," Ryan said. When Cowen got wind of the plan he thought it was typically hare-brained, according to Gogarty. "Cowen saw this as causing problems, he said ... we need uniformity; we need a united Cabinet; this is going to cause trouble." Cowen knew other resignations were on the cards, although he did not say so at the time. Gogarty said the clear message coming from Cowen was: "We need stability at this time. There's some major banking issues coming up ... we need to have everyone on board." Gogarty agreed that the plan, while perhaps well-enough intentioned, was inevitably only going to be interpreted in one way once it was out in the open. "When it started coming out in the media the idea of rotation was kind of like 'jobs for the boys'. That was the angle that was being pushed," he said. "If it was a good Government and the times were good it would have happened seamlessly: it wouldn't have been a problem, but in the economic circumstances it didn't make sense."

The beneficiary of the rotation plan, if it had gone ahead, would have been Cuffe, who criticised the secret nature of the original deal and said the economic situation had a bearing on the Greens' ultimate decision to abandon the plan. "The understanding on going into Government was that there would be a changeover at the halfway stage. Given the extent of the economic difficulties that we were in ... the consensus view within the parliamentary party of the Greens was that it wouldn't be appropriate for the leader to step down from a senior ministry at the half-way point.

As simple as that," he said. Asked if the other senior Minister – Ryan – could have been involved in a rotation, Cuffe said: "The view of the parliamentary party was that it was appropriate for the two senior ministers to continue." It was an unanimous view, he insisted. The original agreement was not made public, which Cuffe thought was a mistake. "There was an agreement between us as a parliamentary party to have that change at the half-way stage. I don't believe it made sense to do it that way, but that was the view at the time." He continued: "I'm happiest when all agreements are public and known to all."

Paul Gogarty argued there was no way the Greens could have survived politically if they had revealed their plan, even to their own members. "The obvious reason why we couldn't tell the party is that if the world knows that John Gormley is going to step down in two-and-a-half years civil servants would play silly buggers," he said. "It's not that you're hiding information, but you can't tell about an agreement like that because you'd be a lame duck Minister." In the event, Cuffe and White were appointed junior Ministers. Cuffe, replacing Sargent, was given the brand new title of Minister of State for Planning, Sustainable Travel and Horticulture. The role certainly played to the former architect and urban planner's strengths. In many ways, it was a "bespoke" ministry, as he described it himself. "It's an area I'm very comfortable with and I thoroughly enjoyed it … I got my dream job." The only downside was spending less time in the modern wing of Leinster House and more in the Department of Transport across the road on Kildare Street. "Actually I loved LH2000 as an office to work in and the move over to the Department of Transport: that was a pig of a building to operate from. You couldn't open the windows and there was a hum of air conditioning, but maybe that was part of Fianna Fáil's cunning plan to grind us down by psychological torture," he joked. It was deemed important for the Greens to put their stamp on a social justice-type Ministry, so White was named Minister of State for Equality, Human Rights and Integration. The position was detached from the Department of Justice, much to the delight of the Greens because of their ongoing difficulties with Dermot Ahern, and tagged on to the Department of Community, Equality and Gaeltacht Affairs. White found her senior Minister Pat Carey allowed her "great leeway" and was "very supportive." In the reshuffle at the end of March, the gentlemanly Carey had been promoted from the Government chief whip's position to take possession of a full Ministry, describing himself as "an overnight success after 25 years in politics." Promoted along with Carey in this cautious reshuffle was Tony Killeen, who became Minister for Defence, while John Curran took over as whip. The Green's senior Ministers retained their portfolios.

However, Gogarty believed he should have been the one to get the new junior Ministerial position, which would have meant all the party's TDs would have tasted Ministerial office. "We were promised by Bertie two senior and two junior [Ministries], with the second junior coming half way through. And the second junior was to be in Education, which was my area … I signed up for a position that I thought was coming down the line," he said. "The way Trevor organised it was that John would be a senior Minister along with Eamon. Eamon would be a senior Minister for five years. John would step down half way through. Mary would become a junior Minister halfway through with Trevor stepping down as a junior. Ciaran would take over from John and I would get the additional junior that comes half way through, so all the parliamentary party would have a ministerial position. That was the agreement," he said "After Stagg it's painted like, Oh Paul Gogarty is the only one who didn't get anything. You couldn't give him anything ... because Paul Gogarty's an eejit. The truth of the matter was I was earmarked for the second junior," he insisted.

Gogarty claimed to have put a compromise proposal to his colleagues when they gathered for a think-in in Clane, Co. Kildare, in January 2010, when consideration was being given to Gormley leaving Cabinet. Gogarty said he also feared Gormley would feel obliged to step down as party leader. "I said, 'Look, our party leader can't resign: it's going to look terrible. We have to think about something else.'" What Gogarty proposed was that he would waive any expectation of a junior ministry. "What I want is that if Ciaran gets [to be] a senior Minister that we push that John would be a super junior and so he'd be in Cabinet," he said. "But I did put a sting in the tail. I said, 'Right, I've made my sacrifice, so to speak.'" Gogarty said also in his mind at that time was a belief that the Government might not last much longer. What, he thought, would be the benefit of becoming a junior Minister for a year and getting nothing done? Pragmatically, he thought a junior Ministerial position would have seen him traipsing the country for far-flung announcements and openings, which would probably have little impact on his Dublin Mid-West constituency and do little to help his re-election chances there. "In hindsight, now that I've lost my seat, it was the money and the parachute and maybe I should have been more selfish," he laughed. "But that's beside the point; that's not why you do things." He claimed to have kept up the pressure on colleagues at parliamentary party meetings over the course of the next few months. "I said, 'I've made my sacrifice guys, what are you going to do? Eamon, what are you going to do? Mary, what are you going to do? Ciaran, what are you going to do? And for the next 10 weeks this issue came up time and time at parliamentary party meetings and no-one budged. No-one was willing to do anything," he said.

"Ciaran was adamant that that was the agreement. He was a senior Minister: that was it," Gogarty claimed. "Eventually Ciaran had to make the noble sacrifice of taking a junior, and we continued on but the party was damaged by it." Many meetings had been dominated by and much time spent on the issue, which wasted a lot of energy that could have been channelled into areas of more value for the party. "It left a sour taste in the mouth because – other people will argue differently – my own take is that is showed a side of the Green Party where people were very much focused on their own positions," Gogarty said.

At the Clane think-in, the Greens tried to keep the focus

on their plans to have a directly-elected mayor for Dublin, with Gormley announcing that the heads of a Bill were now ready to go to Government. The Mayor's wages would be on a par with a Ministerial salary, Gormley revealed. Significant powers in relation to transport, planning and housing would also be involved. Cuffe said friends constantly advised him to tone down the talk about the Mayoral Bill, but he does not regret trying to keep it on the Government's agenda. "Everybody kept telling me to shut up about the Mayoral Bill. I think the Mayoral Bill is crucial for the development of Dublin and every other city around the country," he said. "People would tell me to shut up and stop talking about it ... I so strongly believe in a Mayor for Dublin. I think it's crucial for the management of the city, everything from where the double yellow lines are to the kind of jobs we'll get in Dublin in ten years time. I guess I saw how Barcelona made that happen, how London's using it, so I really believed in it."

Cuffe would have been wise to have heeded the advice of his friends. Fianna Fáil representatives and others could not believe how much time the Greens were prepared to waste, from their perspective, on the initiative. There was disgruntlement too within the Greens, with Gogarty saying the myopic focus on the legislation was one of the party's "fundamental mistakes." He said: "We spent so long on the Mayoralty that we took our eye off the ball on other legislation that might have been more far-reaching, like the Climate Change Bill or even the corporate donations. I think we were being run around by Fianna Fáil, hiding behind the

Attorney General." The Mayoral Bill was a big piece of legislation, which took up a lot of the parliamentary draftsmen's time.

In Clane, Gogarty said he would be interested in campaigning to be Dublin's first elected Mayor. For a time, he thought a "straight-talking, maverick type of role" in the mould of former London mayor Ken Livingstone might suit him. "Because all the media stuff was saying that Paul Gogarty is a muppet, I thought well I better do something that shows me in better standing. So I went to the parliamentary party and I said, 'Listen guys I've made my sacrifice so I think the least you can do is endorse me for Mayor,'" he said. "Now I didn't necessarily want to be Mayor because I saw there was going to be trouble getting the legislation done, but I thought even being touted as a candidate would suggest that I'm not a total eejit who isn't getting anything just because I'm a muppet." However, he later used Twitter to rule himself out of running for the position. "Wish media would focus on issues rather than me as Mayoral candidate. Am NOT running," he tweeted. At one point an exasperated Gogarty said he told colleagues: "Let's ditch the Mayoral stuff and get on to the planning and corporate donations." Others in the party appeared to remain fixated with the legislation, however, perhaps believing it would remain in place as a legacy when the Greens inevitably left or were voted out of Government. They even let it be known that the party was looking for a celebrity candidate to contest the election, which they hoped would take place the following June. They speculated that other parties would field high-profile candidates, perhaps Fine

Gael MEP Gay Mitchell or Labour TD Ruairí Quinn. Rumours persisted at that time that the position was something that might appeal to Bertie Ahern, but he put the kybosh on that theory by complaining publicly about the lack of provision for a Mayoral budget.

Meanwhile, the party's Planning and Development Bill was steadily working its way through the Oireachtas. The party gathered in Waterford for its annual conference, where Gormley's televised leader's speech clashed with Earth Hour, a global event highlighting the impact of climate change. He asked viewers to switch off any unnecessary lights, but not their television sets. Gormley claimed Fine Gael councillors were "still receiving contributions from the developers, still rezoning." The new Bill would put a stop to "unfettered and irresponsible rezonings." Planning problems had begun to raise "their ugly heads" again as a direct consequence of Green Party councillors having been voted off councils the previous June, he claimed. In a frank admission, Gormley told delegates that going into Government was "the biggest reality check that anybody can ever encounter." The impact was akin to a blow from a sledgehammer, he said. "Opposition is for talkers and theorists, you can have it every way." He said he was often asked if he had known the recession was going to be quite so tough, would he have entered Government. "And my answer is clear: 'yes, yes, yes.'"

CHAPTER 9

FOUR LEGS GOOD; TWO LEGS BAD

IN THE MIDDLE OF IRELAND'S ECONOMIC COLLAPSE, A BIZARRE situation arose where the coalition came close to falling apart over dog breeding and stag hunting legislation. A cabal of Fianna Fáil TDs, not normally vocal either in the Dáil or in the media, lined up to berate their own Government's policy and the scale of the revolt shocked senior Ministers and further unpicked the cohesion of the coalition. Angry crowds of rural campaigners, including some on horseback in full hunting regalia, gathered outside Green Party events, with many of them involved in a newly-formed organisation called Rural Ireland Says Enough! (RISE!). Any time a compromise appeared to be reached between Brian Cowen and John Gormley, it was invariably leaked to the media, driving Cowen to fury at Fianna Fáil parliamentary party meetings.

It should have come as no surprise to Fianna Fáil backbenchers that the Green Party was interested in promoting animal welfare legislation, but still the junior coalition partner's efforts left them feeling more than a little disgruntled. Fianna Fáil deputies had often grumbled about 'the tail wagging the dog' throughout the life of the Coalition Government, but now there was a genuine sense of being pushed in an objectionable policy direction among rural TDs from the larger party. The Green grassroots, on the other hand, felt what they regarded as progress had been painfully slow and were disappointed in what they saw as the leadership's lack of assertiveness on these core issues. The leader John Gormley and his deputy Mary White, the Green's only rural-based TD, bore the brunt of criticism from both sides.

As a child who spent a lot of time in the countryside, White herself had run with the Wicklow hunting pack, the Bray Harriers, "with my little yellow plaits on my pony called Lucky." But her perception of the past-time changed as the years passed. "I loved it, but then I grew up and I didn't think chasing a live animal to kill it was great." White claimed the pieces of legislation to ban stag hunting with hounds and regulate dog breeding establishments that proved so contentious were in fact "peripheral" to the Green's agenda in Government, yet many people with an attachment to traditional rural pursuits had become convinced the party wanted to take things further. "When John came down to open the new library in Borris [Co. Carlow] we had eggs thrown at us by my friends and neighbours who thought that we were going to stop hunting and fishing and shooting," she said. *The Irish Times'* report of that day in late June 2010 said eggs were put inside the interior of Gormley's State car and placed on the bonnet, though none were thrown.

While the very concept of hunting obviously upset many Greens, White insisted the party had never been opposed to shooting or fishing, as some protesters were alleging, "because you fish to eat and you shoot to eat, and you're not pursuing a live animal by another live animal; setting animal on animal." The perception was proving unshakable, however. "It was just part of the popular myth that 'the Greens have lost it', and that was very painful to have eggs thrown at you in your own town … It was a bandwagon of misinformation, and I think purposefully misconstrued, that we were going to do all these things despite us saying that we weren't," White said.

Gormley had taken a fair amount of flak back in October 2009, when his spokesman was forced to clarify that the Minister for the Environment remained staunchly opposed to stag hunting despite having issued a licence to the Ward Union Hunt in Co. Meath, Ireland's only stag hunt. The Green's old adversary, Fine Gael TD Shane McEntee, welcomed the move, describing the hunt as a "vital component" of the rural community, but he could not resist a jibe at the Minister. "I understand that a ban on stag hunting remains a key objective for the Green Party … So I can only assume that Minister Gormley has had a change of heart on this matter," McEntee said mischievously.

Gormley's spokesman insisted the Minister, both in Opposition and in Government, had been outspoken and firm in his opposition to stag hunting, but refusing to issue the licence to what was the only licensed hunt in the country would require legislative change.

This embarrassment appeared to light a fire under Gormley, however, and the following month he was able to confirm that a ban on deer hunting using hounds was genuinely a step closer after Cabinet approved the heads of a Bill which would make it an offence. An amendment to the 1976 and 2000 Wildlife Acts would include a provision prohibiting deer hunting with a hound or pack of hounds, a move which he stressed was not intended to have implications for pursuits such as fox hunting, hare coursing and the shooting of deer. In an attempt to placate their political opponents, the Greens attempted to package the decision as having been taken more on the grounds of public safety than on the basis of animal welfare. "One of the reports I received … showed deer going across the road just in front of a car. That set off alarm bells for me, and it seemed to me that licensing this was just not feasible, particularly in a built-up, increasingly urbanised area, and that's why I came to this conclusion," Gormley contended.

Bringing about an end to stag-hunting was by now a solid commitment in the programme for government which had been renegotiated between Fianna Fáil and the Greens. The proposed change to the Animal Welfare Acts also included new powers for the Minister to make regulations to prohibit or regulate the use of jet-skis, quad bikes, scramblers and off-road 4x4 vehicles in environmentally-sensitive locations. Controversies around such activities had arisen in locations such as Lough Derravaragh in

Co. Westmeath, Mount Leinster and the Slieve Bloom Mountains. Exemptions would of course be made for farmers using such vehicles in the course of their daily work, Gormley stressed. Gormley said he was amending the legislation to address issues "in relation to which Ireland is at present under pressure from the European Commission on foot of judgments of the European Court of Justice," because Ireland had failed to address the impact of recreational activities that were detrimental to specially protected areas of conservation across the country. "We wanted to make sure that we are not disturbing birds or harming protected flora and fauna," he explained. Financial penalties for Wildlife Acts breaches would increase for the first time in almost a decade under the legislation, having last been amended in the 2000 Act. A breach which would have incurred a fine of €500 would now result in a €1,000 penalty, for instance. The Minister also gave himself new powers to prohibit and regulate the importation, transport and sale of what he called "invasive" species, such as African pond weed, wild rhododendron, zebra mussel and grey squirrel.

The other piece of animal-related legislation the Greens faced a challenge on from their Fianna Fáil colleagues was the so-called 'puppy farm' Bill or the Dog Breeding Establishments Bill, to give the proposed law its correct title. White said this legislation "was simply to stop these awful puppy farms where you have these poor bitches just having litter upon litter upon litter." The Bill was intended to give a legislative basis for the regulation of the operation of dog-breeding establishments. It would require local authorities to establish and maintain registers of establishments and prohibit the operation of those that were unregistered. It was also meant to provide for an increase in fees for dog licences, as well as some other amendments to the Control of Dogs Acts 1986-1992. Bodies representing some dog breeders, as well as hunting organisations, lobbied Fianna Fáil Oireachtas members on the proposed legislation. The breeders' objected to several points including the extent of the increase in dog licence fees and the levels of penalties that could be imposed for breaches of the proposed legislation, as well as the circumstances under which dogs would be micro-chipped.

No Green had ever set foot in the hallowed parliamentary party rooms of Fianna Fáil, but dog breeding was deemed so important and so contentious that Gormley was invited to come up to the fifth floor of Leinster House for the first time in February 2010 to discuss the proposed legislation. Much to his surprise, Gormley was applauded as he entered the spacious conference room adorned with imposing pictures of former Fianna Fáil leaders. A motion tabled by one of the Fianna Fáil TDs who shared White's Carlow-Kilkenny constituency, Bobby Aylward, called for amendments to the Bill "where dog breeders will be severely affected by the financial and legal obligations as currently proposed." Confident of support from a number of rural TDs and Senators, Aylward stuck a conciliatory tone, saying he agreed with the Bill in principle, and stressing measures to eradicate abuse of dogs were required, but adding that he viewed other proposals as "very severe." He said he hoped Gormley would look sympathetically on his request for amendments. Concluding his little speech, Aylward found that he couldn't resist the old gag: "We're in Government together and you have to get on, but it can't be a case of the tail wagging the dog, if you'll excuse the pun." There was no laughter from Gormley, who felt he had right on his side. He countered that the proposed legislation would stop "backstreet dog-breeders" and also be of benefit to those commercial breeders who did a good job and treated their animals well. It was a highly emotive issue for the Greens, as Gormley knew all too well, and any weakening of the legislation would undoubtedly hurt the party's core vote.

At the end of March 2010, as the Greens gathered in Waterford for their annual convention, furious rural campaigners flocked there too and filled the streets outside the hotel. The Greens had expected a protest, although perhaps not all of them had anticipated the size it would be. "We did see it coming. I remember Liam Reid saying, 'This is gonna be big,'" said Ciaran Cuffe. It would not have been wise for a Green politician to step outside the door for a number of hours that day. Angry protesters jeered Gormley after he was derided by a man with a megaphone as "a fella on a bicycle in Dublin telling you how to run a farm." Inside the convention, Gormley insisted: "We are a party that is committed to maintaining rural life." The Green leader said he understood the protestors' complaints to be centred on Green-sponsored legislation on planning, stag hunting, dog breeding and turf cutting. The party wanted to end the traditional practice of turf cutting on designated raised bogs as part of its plan to accelerate the transition away from the extraction of turf altogether, which was not going down well in rural areas either. The protesters made no secret of their intention to lobby Fianna Fáil backbenchers aggressively against these pieces of legislation. At the conference, there was a frank acknowledgement that the Green organisation, in electoral terms, remained an urban rather than a rural movement. As deputy leader and by then newly-appointed Minister of State Mary White stressed in her conference address, she was "the only rural TD in this party." In constituencies outside the capital, such as White's of Carlow-Kilkenny, anti-Green lobbying would become most rigorous. The party's deputy leader was dubbed a "dangerous woman" by rural campaigners.

"People thought we were hooked on banning stags and hooked on the Dog Breeding Establishment Bill, but the stag Bill was two pages, if I remember, and it was brought in because of safety issues," White said. "Stag hunting: I mean, I'm not into hunting at all, but stag hunting which was now in an urban environment, is a no-no. So it was simply an issue of public safety … It's not a wild stag it's cruel to hunt a domestic animal, let it out in the wild, and then grown men throw themselves on the stag at the end of the day put it back in a horse box and bring it out again in a few weeks time when it's recovered from that trauma." The Greens' concerns were being used against them, White argued. She acknowledged that the Fianna Fáil TDs who rose up against the Green-sponsored legislation were doing so because they were getting it in the neck from their constituents. She was hearing the same thing, obviously.

Purely from an optics point of view, the timing of these pieces of legislation passing through the Houses of the Oireachtas was pitifully bad, "at a time when people were having pension levies and losing their jobs," as White conceded. Despite the communications team's best efforts, the Greens became vulnerable to the accusation that they were more interested in animals than they were in people. "In fact the Greens wanted to make sure that we had a country that we could all live in and draw salaries in and have a bit of social justice. The stags and the dogs were peripheral," White said.

By the time the Cabinet eventually approved the Bill to ban stag hunting at the end of March 2010, the disgruntled rural Fianna Fáil backbenchers appeared to have as good as given up complaining about it and the matter lay dormant for a while, but they continued to claim Gormley had "snubbed" their concerns about the dog-breeding legislation. Gormley had received a cordial reception when he spoke to the Fianna Fáil parliamentary party about the dog breeding legislation, and was invited back to address members of Fianna Fáil's environmental policy group. But with tensions escalating between the coalition partners, the meeting did not take place as planned. Some Fianna Fáil representatives gathering in the party's rooms knew beforehand that Gormley would not attend, while others said they only found out when they arrived at the meeting. Gormley's spokesman said the Minister had wanted two officials to be in attendance, but did not believe it was correct to bring them to the Fianna Fáil party rooms. He offered to meet a small Fianna Fáil delegation in his own office but this offer was rebuffed and the meeting was rescheduled for the following day in a neutral meeting room in Leinster House. It had been one of the busiest days of the political year, dominated by developments relating to the National Asset Management Agency (Nama), but an air of unreality had taken hold in Leinster House. Cork South-West TD Christy O'Sullivan fumed about his disappointment at Gormley's no-show at the Fianna Fáil meeting. "He snubbed us in this way," O'Sullivan said. Demonstrating how hostile relations between the Coalition partners had become, Tipperary South deputy Mattie McGrath said: "We weren't going to belittle ourselves by going down to him ... He's been in before and we treated him civilly."

An hour-long meeting did take place on March 31, in Leinster House's audio-visual room, with the Minister accompanied by three officials from the Department of the Environment. Afterwards, Gormley said he would consider the possibility of varying some details of the dog breeding Bill following the meeting with rural Fianna Fáil backbenchers. They had called for amendments to the Bill which they believed would be welcomed by the greyhound industry, the Hunting Association of Ireland and the Canine Breeders of Ireland. Gormley's spokesman struck a note of scepticism about their concerns that day.

"The Minister believes much of the concerns are based on misunderstandings and misinformation. However, he has agreed to look at the possibility of varying some details as the Bill progresses," he said. Laois-Offaly TD Seán Fleming, who was among some 20 Fianna Fáil representatives in attendance, said he believed both sides found the meeting useful, but emphasised the distance between the two parties. "The Minister is a city-based Minister. I'm saying that as a matter of fact rather than criticism. He wouldn't have grown up with the issue in the way some Fianna Fáil TDs would have. We hope by the time the Bill comes into the Dáil he will probably be able to announce some changes." Waterford deputy Brendan Kenneally said he would like those involved in the greyhound industry and people who bred dogs for hunting to be exempt from the Bill. While he was not sure this would be possible, he hoped an "acceptable sort of way" forward would be found.

On Monday 12 April the Taoiseach Brian Cowen faced a noisy reception from pro-hunt campaigners in Roscrea, Co. Tipperary. Participants in the demonstration organised by RISE! whistled, jeered and even shouted "Tally ho!" as the Taoiseach arrived to perform the official opening of a leisure centre. While RISE! spokesman Joe Griffin said about 200 people attended, a Garda spokesman said 50-60 people were present. People involved in fox hunting, greyhound racing, deerstalking, coursing and gun clubs were represented at the protest. Griffin said hundreds of jobs depended on the continuation of such pursuits. Not one to mince his words, he said the demonstrators wanted to "stop these ludicrous Greens ramming home their fundamentalist policies." The perception that the issue was one of concern only to rural people was incorrect, he said, pointing out that Green chairman Senator Dan Boyle from Cork, was "seeking to get elected where there are thousands of hunters in his constituency."

Significantly, Cowen plainly told reporters that day that Fianna Fáil did not disagree with the Green Party on the issue of stag hunting, and he moved to clarify that the proposed legislation, which would make hunting deer with a pack of hounds an offence, would not affect other pursuits. "There isn't an issue between the Coalition partners on the fact that there is a Bill, as you know, coming forward in relation to stag hunting, which in no way affects the wider issue of country pursuits generally. I'd like to make that clear," he told reporters. "There has been some indication from some people that it represents a wider issue than the actual specific issue we're dealing with, and it doesn't." But Cowens words were by now falling on deaf ears.

As May continued, the level of bitterness between Fianna Fáil and Green Oireachtas members was reaching new heights, as they clashed in public over the Dog Breeding Establishments Bill at a packed environment committee meeting. Fianna Fáil TD for Kerry South John O'Donoghue, a former Ceann Comhairle, said there was concern among rural dwellers the proposed legislation was going to lead to further legislative measures that would "interfere with if not destroy" country pursuits. "There's a feeling out there in the countryside among those involved in pursuits of a rural nature ... that this legislation, whilst welcome in some respects, is the thin end of the wedge," he said.

O'Donoghue said while he did not believe Gormley wished to "sow doubt in people's minds", the Green Party leader also had a "duty" to reassure rural dwellers about their hobbies.

Emboldened perhaps by this intervention from such a senior Fianna Fáil figure, Tipperary North TD Máire Hoctor said backbenchers had not been consulted about a ban on stag hunting contained in the programme for government. Hoctor claimed the "preference" of the Greens was to ban other forms of hunting, adding: "That's not part of a programme for government I'm part of." When McGrath suggested some animal welfare activists were "nothing short of terrorists", Trevor Sargent showed his mettle and firmly said he took exception to the inference. "We're implementing a programme for government that was agreed. End of story," Sargent said. Responding to the suggestion from a number of Fianna Fáil TDs that the 1958 Greyhound Industry Act could be amended rather than new legislation introduced, Sargent said statistics indicated it was not adequate. Mark Deary backed Sargent up: "There is no big Green agenda here ... it does what it says on the tin. It's a Bill to regulate dog breeding establishments ... to try to present it as the thin end of the wedge is disingenuous." Fine Gael TD Tom Hayes called on Gormley to make a statement to the Dáil in the next few days to attempt to alleviate people's concerns, while Hayes' party colleague McEntee said "it was wrong to even touch stag hunting."

As tensions continued, Cowen asked Gormley to tweak proposed amendments to the dog-breeding legislation to satisfy rural Fianna Fáil backbenchers threatening to vote against it. The matter kept coming up at increasingly fractious meetings of the Fianna Fáil parliamentary party, and there was by now some level of concern within the Coalition about the voting intentions of McGrath and, at that stage, Hoctor. Gormley wrote to Cowen on 26 May outlining a "suite of amendments" concerning micro-chipping, inspections, fees and breeding limitations, along with a "review clause" to examine the impact on the greyhound industry 12 months after the law had been introduced. The Green Party leader characterised the amendments as "a significant concession on my part", and Cowen went ballistic at a parliamentary party meeting after the letter was leaked to *The Irish Times*. A small group of Fianna Fáil backbenchers continued to seek clarifications on some amendments and demanded further changes on others. Aylward highlighted fees and the definition of a breeding bitch as particular concerns. "We need clarification before we vote on it. You don't buy a pig in a poke. We have to carry our own people as well as the Greens on this one," he warned. O'Sullivan said the proposed legislation should not be rushed. "If it takes longer than what's being anticipated by the Minister to get these issues resolved then so be it."

Meanwhile, Rise! was planning a demonstration outside Leinster House to coincide with the upcoming debate on the legislation in the Dáil. Separately, Fianna Fáil grandee Eamon Ó Cuív, a grandson of the party founder Eamon de Valera, struck an ominous note in an interview with *The Irish Times* when he said the unease felt by some rural people about proposed legislation to regulate dog breeding reminded him of the biggest political storm of his career, which followed "the proposal to impose a very modest rod licence to fishermen in Lough Corrib." That bitter row had torn his community apart, he recalled. Ó Cuív had now become the most senior Fianna Fáil person to intervene in the row when he said the Dog Breeding Establishments Bill should be examined for "unintended consequences."

Ó Cuív spoke in soothing terms when he said he knew the Greens did not have "ulterior motives", but he did refer to a fear in rural Ireland that pursuits that had been enjoyed for generations were suddenly going to be stopped. "The absolute agreement is the stag hunt is to cease, and we're legislating for that, and that all the other country pursuits can continue … the Dog Bill of course is about standards and so on, it's about a different issue, but obviously people are worried about the implications and it's a good idea in my view to look into this very carefully to make sure there are no unintended consequences out of it," he said. "I don't think any Fianna Fáil person has any reservations in relation to eliminating any cruelty or mishandling of dogs or whatever. What they feel is there might be unintended consequences out of the legislation, particularly in relation to keeping greyhounds, hunting dogs and so on, and I think they're concerned to make sure there aren't any unintended consequences." Ó Cuív was keen to stress his understanding of both rural and urban points of view, saying he was always amazed at the number of people "who think I'm pure country" when around half of his life had been spent in Dublin. "The first half of my life was pure city upbringing, pure 100 per cent middle-class Dublin upbringing. And the other half of my life has been living in a very rural area, in a really rural, rural area, and I am very much made up of those two halves. There's part of me that is, I would hope, very much in tune with rural Ireland."

In June, panic struck the Greens when Fine Gael claimed the junior coalition partner's Bills had been dropped from the Government's agenda, after Fine Gael TD Phil Hogan (who would become Minister for the Environment in 2011) said proposed legislation relating to stag hunting, dog breeding and other matters did not appear on a list circulated between party whips. He pointed to an interview Gormley gave to *The Irish Times* that very week, in which the Green leader had said the dog and stag Bills would be passed before the summer recess. "Even the least sharp-eyed Green Party supporter can see that those Bills are nowhere on the Government's list. It's clear that Fianna Fáil have stalled the Green Party agenda in Government," Hogan scoffed. He revealed the Department of the Taoiseach had e-mailed the party whips a list of nine Bills it was hoped would come before the House before the summer recess. The Bills listed on the e-mail referred to by Hogan related to: merchant shipping, health, carbon, social welfare, Údarás Na Gaeltachta, head shops, prescriptions and roads. The Health Miscellaneous Provisions Bill and the Health Amendment Bill were also mentioned. The Green-sponsored Bills were nowhere to be seen, however. Labour Party whip Emmet Stagg too said no effort had been made to inform him the Green-sponsored legislation would come before the Dáil. "It's very strange. There was an extensive interview with the leader of the Greens only a few days ago in which he said how important they [the Bills] were, and none of them have appeared," he added. The Government claimed Hogan was wrong and Fianna Fáil and the Greens were working together to fulfil all of their legislative commitments. Fine Gael stood accused of distributing a partial internal document which was for circulation strictly between the whips of the various parties. A spokesman for the Green Party said the matter had been clarified to the party's satisfaction. "These things are on the list," he said.

Fianna Fáil Senator Denis O'Donovan abstained in the Seanad vote on the proposed dog breeding legislation, describing the amendments proposed by Gormley as "weak." An unlikely rebel, O'Donovan, from Bantry in Co. Cork, had been a prominent backbencher in the previous administration and chairman of the all-party committee on the Constitution. He said: "I'm taking a stance for rural Ireland and rural pursuits ... Seven or eight critical amendments would save the day. He [Gormley] is making moves but it's more like shadow boxing than landing a proper punch."

The trio leading the charge against the Green legislation – Hoctor, O'Sullivan and McGrath – were spotted huddled together and plotting their next move in the Dáil members' bar one night. The Dáil record would soon show whether there was posturing going on in an attempt to impress rural voters in Tipperary North, Cork South-West and Tipperary South, or if this apparently minor piece of legislation was truly a flashpoint between the Coalition partners.

CHAPTER 10

'THEY WANT TO STOP THE PUSSYCAT GOING AFTER THE MOUSE'

WHILE THE GRUMBLING RURAL FIANNA FÁIL BACKBENCHERS HAD been widely dismissed in political circles as dogs who would not bark, their threatened rebellion turned out to be very real in this instance. The extent of the relentless media focus on the conflict between elements of the Fianna Fáil and Green parties on animal welfare legislation had become frustrating for Green handlers, keen to position the party as heavily involved in attempts to rectify the economy and banking sector, rather than married to niche policy areas. But when seven Fianna Fáil TDs lined up to speak out in the Dáil chamber against their own Government's legislation to ban stag hunting on 24 June 2010, they proved the story was not a media construct.

With further Green Party-inspired animal welfare legislation due to come before the Dáil the following week, Ministers were finally getting the message that the cohesion of the Coalition would be sorely tested before the summer recess – if indeed the Government lasted that long. A dismayed-looking John Gormley sat in the chamber listening as a string of Fianna Fáil speakers denounced the ban on stag hunting during an ill-tempered debate following the introduction of the Bill in the Dáil the previous day. Of the eight Fianna Fáil TDs who spoke during the second stage debate, only one, Minister of State Martin Mansergh, a former adviser to three taoisigh who proudly described himself as a part-time farmer, could find it in his heart to back the Bill at this very late stage.

Three of the Fianna Fáil TDs for Meath expressed outright opposition to the legislation affecting the Ward Union Hunt, based in Co. Meath and in north Co. Dublin. Thomas Byrne from Meath East even questioned the constitutionality of the legislation and went as far as to suggest that President Mary McAleese should refer it to the Council of State. Meath West's Johnny Brady warned the Minister, the Taoiseach and other members of the Government "that they cannot depend on my support whether this Government lasts two months or two years … if anything else is tinkered with you have not my support." Mary Wallace represented Meath East along with Byrne, although the pair did not get on. She said the ban was a threat to the rural economy and she had deep reservations about it, while Dublin North TD Michael Kennedy said there should be an impact assessment undertaken on the issue.

Fine Gael's Shane McEntee pleaded with the Minister to defer the Bill in more colourful terms, saying there would be more blood spilled in Croke Park on the upcoming Sunday when Dublin played Meath than there would be in ten years of the Ward Hunt. Responding, Gormley said the decision to introduce the legislation had not been taken lightly and insisted there were public safety issues involved, as it was simply not possible for the hunt to prevent deer in flight from leaping through hedges on to public roads. The Minister then turned his rising ire on Labour, attacking that party for its unexpected opposition to the Bill. In a headline writers dream, the Labour whip Emmet Stagg was among a number of Labour TDs who confirmed they did not support a stag hunting ban. The Irish Council Against Blood Sports said it was horrified to learn that Labour leader Eamon Gilmore was listed as a member in Nealon's Guide to the 30th Dáil.

Gormley told the Dáil he was not surprised at Fine Gael's attitude but was "disappointed at the cynical decision by the Labour Party to abandon its opposition to blood sports." He said senior members of the party, including Gilmore and former leaders Pat Rabbitte and Ruairí Quinn, had publicly stated their opposition to stag hunting and other such practices. "It appears that for Labour Party members, no principle is too cherished to be abandoned if they believe there are votes in it for them." Michael D Higgins declared it was outrageous to suggest Labour favoured cruelty or blood sports. Meanwhile, as had been expected, the party whip was removed from Fianna Fáil Senator Denis O'Donovan for abstaining in the Seanad vote on the Dog Breeding Establishment Bill the previous week.

On 29 June, a series of crucial votes on the stag hunting legislation began, with a meeting of the Fianna Fáil parliamentary party taking place more or less simultaneously. The meeting started at 5.30 pm and was interrupted by two votes on the legislation under discussion. Brian Cowen, in common with others, could barely believe so much precious time and energy was being spent on the matter at such a serious juncture in the State's economic history. He angrily dismissed Tipperary South TD Mattie McGrath's claim that the Green Party was "bullying" Fianna Fáil. Strong criticism of Gormley was voiced by Cork South West deputy Christy O'Sullivan. Wallace, previously one of the most vocal critics of the Bill, backed down and said that in spite of her strong objections to the legislation she would not vote against it as she did not want to be instrumental in the fall of the Government. "But never again will I support an ideological sop to our minority partners, the Green Party, who blatantly don't understand the realities of rural life," she declared. It was not a comfortable gathering. Limerick West TD Niall Collins told the meeting: "We can't be getting soft and rolling over on the Wildlife Bill and be seen as capitulating to the Bailey brothers and Johnny Ronans and big builders and the Dublin 4 set that ride out with the Ward Union."

When the Fianna Fáil TDs trooped down to the chamber for the first vote, both McGrath and O'Sullivan abstained. Cowen was furious. When the Fianna Fáil meeting resumed immediately afterwards, a stern-faced Cowen read from a copy of the rules of the party and gave the clear impression that anyone who abstained or sided with the Opposition in the next vote would lose the whip. Cowen commended his party's deputies from Meath for backing the legislation, despite intense lobbying from pro-hunting groups, and others praised them for their loyalty to the party. The two rebels came under huge pressure from their colleagues to back the legislation.

With 15 minutes to go until the second and final vote at 7 pm, Clare TD Timmy Dooley intervened with a proposal suggesting that Cowen should go to a side room with McGrath and O'Sullivan to discuss the issue privately. The notion did not go down well with Cowen. In fact he rejected it immediately, thundering that he had no intention of getting into a "huddle" with anyone. "We're all men enough to do our business here in the parliamentary party room," he said. The discussion continued and after a short time Cowen said: "We are going down to vote and I expect people to vote for the party." As one observer described Cowen's attitude: "It was: this is it – my way or the highway."

There were further dramatic scenes in the Dáil before the final vote as Fianna Fáil TDs, oblivious to the astonished looks of political opponents and reporters, clustered around McGrath and O'Sullivan and pleaded with them to vote for the Bill. Upping the stakes, Fine Gael had withdrawn the 'pairing' arrangement it had provided in earlier votes on the basis that the position had changed due to the Fianna Fáil abstentions. Under the arrangement, a Fine Gael deputy would stand down for any votes taken in a Fianna Fáil deputy's unavoidable absence.

McGrath voted against the Government in the final vote,

and was immediately expelled from the parliamentary party, while O'Sullivan toed the line and sided with the Coalition. The Government managed to survive the crucial vote and the Bill was passed by 75 votes to 72 in an electronic vote with McGrath voting with the Opposition and then by 75 to 71 in a walk-through vote in which the Tipperary TD abstained. Significantly, two Independent TDs Michael Lowry and Jackie Healy Rae, who had consistently backed the Government since 2007, now saw which way the political wind was blowing and voted against the Bill with both claiming it was an attack on country pursuits and rural life.

By dramatically siding with Fianna Fáil's political opponents in the final division, McGrath became the fifth member of the parliamentary party to lose the whip since the last election. An unrepentant McGrath immediately declared he would vote against the dog breeding legislation the following week. "It should be shredded. It's in no Programme for Government," McGrath declared, comically adding: "Green people want to close the zoo, want to stop horseracing, they want to stop the pussycat going after the mouse." McGrath's frequently-quoted line drove the Greens crazy, with Mary White still spitting fury about "that kind of nonsense." Fianna Fáil was not the only party to have problems on the stag Bill, incidentally. Labour TD Tommy Broughan, a long-time opponent of blood sports, absented himself from the final vote on the measure and Stagg swiftly wrote to Broughan, telling him he had lost the party whip as a result of his abstention.

The exhausting power struggles over animal welfare

legislation had provided an unexpected twist to the Dáil term and left the Greens wondering if the associated stress had been even remotely worth it. The autobiography of former British prime minister Tony Blair, *The Journey*, was released around that time and in it he revealed the contentious fox-hunting Bill was one of the parliamentary measures he most regretted getting involved in, and frankly admitted not knowing enough about the debate at the time. The "primeval" passions aroused by the issue in Britain shocked Blair. "By the end of it, I felt like the damn fox," he wrote. Something similar had happened in Ireland and Gormley felt just as weary as Blair had done: he knew voters had already decided to hunt down his Green pack and pick them off one by one.

Dan Boyle contended the Fianna Fáil backbench rebellion was somewhat manufactured. He remained unconvinced that the revolt was genuine and felt backbenchers in the senior coalition party were in fact encouraged to speak out of turn.

"I think it was fermented to a certain extent. I think people were allowed to have a free rein … there were nods and winks, not direct – you go out and do this and you embarrass the Greens," Boyle said. "Heads were thrust up over the parapet and nothing happened. There wasn't going to be discipline used against them and they weren't threatened with not being candidates … and people acted with abandon." It was the Fianna Fáil backbenchers, rather than the Greens, who chose to make an issue of the stag hunting legislation, Boyle said. "We expected it to go through on the nod. We expected it was a simple piece of legislation that was part of the programme for government and no-one should have had any problem with it." Boyle said the Greens at that time were prioritising the Planning Bill and the Civil Partnership Bill, but that was not reflected in the media coverage. "It was a classic piece of spinning against us that stuck," he said. The Rise! Campaign was masterminded by Liam Cahill, an experienced communications consultant who would end up being hired on a contract basis by Fine Gael's McEntee when the Meath East TD was appointed a junior minister by Enda Kenny. Cahill ran a highly effective campaign that the Greens found practically impossible to counteract and he would later claim that in the 2011 general election, "we saw off Gormley and the Green agenda from political life."

The episode was particularly difficult for urban Greens, with Paul Gogarty protesting that the legislation that provoked such debate was practically irrelevant in his Dublin Mid-West electoral area. "It didn't figure; it was never a big issue in my constituency but it was just used to fulfil a narrative about what the Greens were, which wasn't a true narrative," he said. "I'm a vegetarian, I don't wear leather, I don't eat meat but I never put anything about vegetarianism in my political leaflets, anything about animal rights, even climate change to a degree didn't figure much because I felt people don't really care about it," he added. "If you can educate them about issues well and good but I think you try and do stuff in Government on those issues, but if you just rant on those issues you're not going to get elected." He insisted the Greens had a wider agenda, but were unable to communicate this. "So when we made our stag and our little animal rights stand, it was a small piece of legislation. We saw it as part of a much wider agenda but elements within the media and particularly the organised campaign by Rise! and some Fianna Fáil, Fine Gael and Labour deputies painted it like this was the big idea of the Green Party, this was all we were concerned about and we were now going to dismantle rural Ireland and stop people hunting and fishing and engaging in decent rural pursuits."

Ciaran Cuffe too despaired at the media focus on the legislation and remains furious with what he called the "quite fancy PR" employed by opponents of the Greens. "I think an awful lot of what were seen to be mistakes were more interpretation and the emphases that were put on our actions by the media in particular," he said. "Whenever anyone says, 'Ah you spent lots of time on stags and hares', I say, 'I didn't; I don't believe that John Gormley did', but it suited certain elements in the media to perpetuate certain stereotypes about the Greens and that's always been the case." He continued: "It's been sandal wearing Greens from the word go 29 years ago. I don't think I've ever worn sandals to the Dáil or to a city council meeting but for whatever reasons some people like stereotypes to persist and if you learned everything from one or two media outlets you'd think we spent hours in conclave discussing exactly what a greyhound a stag or a hare could or couldn't do and that wasn't the case."

Cuffe said "the environmental message" had always been a difficult one to sell and once a view took hold it could be very hard to shift. There were backbenchers in both Fianna Fáil and Fine Gael "who love to make suggestions about what the Greens wanted to do to rural Ireland," he added. This occurred "over very simple issues like the nitrates directive, where we wanted to ensure that rivers were clean and our fishing was protected and we weren't facing daily fines from Brussels." But Cuffe claimed the Green's opponents across the political divide found it easier to get headlines in their local newspapers by criticising the Greens.

Cuffe said wider debates about the future of rural Ireland were all too often dominated by vested interests, and the Greens frequently found themselves fighting a losing battle. "You're talking about rural Ireland when family farms have been decimated; when the amount of full-time farmers fell dramatically over the last ten or 20 years. And to say, 'No there are ways we can keep people on the land other than simply beef cattle,' it's a hard message to communicate." Mary White too, as has been stated, believed the impact of the animal welfare legislation was "blown out of all proportion." In common with many Greens, she believed the party was the victim of a "very good, well funded, targeted campaign of vilification against the Greens, no question."

AT THE END OF SEPTEMBER 2010, A FUNDRAISING DINNER celebrating the party's legislative achievements in animal welfare was moved from Leinster House to another venue. Trying to raise money in Leinster House was not the done thing, the Greens were advised, and they also wanted to avoid accusations of gloating at Fianna Fáil and rural campaigners. Mark Deary said it was time to try "healing divisions, not exaggerating them." The event was a sell-out, apparently. Tickets cost €55, with proceeds going towards the party's "ongoing work to end cruelty to animals." The four-course fish and vegetarian menu featured Cashel blue gateaux with pickled pears or lentil and bean soup for starters, a main course of galette of wild mushroom or baked salmon with cucumber and mint, and dark chocolate mousse with Irish Mist for dessert. At the dinner, Gormley referred to the Government's next piece of animal welfare legislation, the Animal Health and Welfare Bill, the heads of which were described as being at an advanced stage in the Department of Agriculture and expected to be submitted to Government soon. In December, greyhound breeding legislation, which caused such tensions between the Government parties in the summer that it had to be taken out of the dog breeding bill, was quietly agreed by the Cabinet.

Animal welfare legislation was generally speaking the responsibility of the Department of Agriculture, and the Fianna Fáil Minister for Agriculture Brendan Smith said he did not think differences between Fianna Fáil and the Green Party over animal welfare legislation damaged relations between the coalition partners. He was franker in his view of some of the campaigning pro-hunting groups, however. "There was a lot of misrepresentation in relation to the issues that came before the Dáil … There were people campaigning against those legislative measures that were not addressing the particular issues at all," he said. "They were putting out scare-mongering stories that fishing would be banned, that hunting would be banned and that all rural pursuits would be banned. That was absolutely disingenuous and it was not factual. That would generate antagonism to any political party or to any individual minister or public representative as well."

Come September 2010, the Greens were being frank about just how difficult a general election was going to be for them. An increasingly angry electorate had already demonstrated its determination to punish the junior Coalition partner severely in the local and European elections of 2009. The Greens now knew for certain that seats would be lost at the next general election. Survival as a political entity had been as much as they had dared dream of for quite some time, and now they were going so far as to say so in public. "The Green Party fully accepts any election between now and summer 2012 is going to be a very difficult election for them," the party's spokesman in Government said at the time.

Relations with Coalition partners Fianna Fáil were now characterised as "workmanlike" by the plain-speaking Trevor Sargent. While the Government was due to run until 2012, no-one believed it would anymore and the fluctuating political temperature meant an election could take place sooner than either of the Government partners had ever previously anticipated. The Greens attempted to adopt a "head-down" approach to what remained of their time in office, with a focus firmly on the economy and policy.

But in rural areas dislike of Gormley in particular had reached unprecedented levels which surprised his loyal supporters in the party and he was constantly derided for being out of touch with country life. Gormley loyalist Paul Gogarty hit the nail on the head at the time. "I think there's a narrative out there that the Greens are about taxing people and we care more about animals than people. It's not true and it's totally unfair," he said. "John Gormley has become a hate figure in some circles. He's been portrayed as the Michael McDowell of the Green Party." Gogarty admitted the Greens had by now adopted a "besieged" mentality in Government. "We're not at war with each other and not at war with Fianna Fáil. But we are perplexed at how to communicate we are more interested in people than animals, and not in trying to tax people for the fun of it."

At the beginning of July, last-minute negotiations continued at the highest levels of the Fianna Fáil and Green parties in order to shore-up support for the dog-breeding legislation, which was just about to be debated in the Dáil, in order to avoid a repeat of the embarrassing debacle surrounding the stag hunting law. As a compromise measure it was agreed that the particularly contentious elements of the dog breeding Bill relating to the greyhound industry would be dealt with later in an amended version of the 1958 Greyhound Industry Act. Fianna Fáil's O'Sullivan and Máire Hoctor of Tipperary North lobbied for the Hunting Association of Ireland (HAI) to be exempt from the legislation, but this was not permitted. Despite the unexpected uprising over the last piece of legislation, Government sources insisted they were confident the Bill would pass, with a spokesman for the Government Chief Whip saying: "We're working towards a consensus."

But McGrath had already confirmed he would vote against the Bill, saying he believed Gormley would "let the hunting people go to hell", and a small group of Fianna Fáil backbenchers continued to claim their support could not be guaranteed. The Greens attempted to counter McGrath's argument, insisting that the "hunting people" he referred to were benefiting from numerous advantages and changes to the legislation as originally proposed. The outspoken Fianna Fáil TD John McGuinness of Carlow-Kilkenny joined with O'Sullivan and Hoctor in insisting Gormley had given a previous commitment that groups affiliated to the HAI be granted a total exemption from the requirements of the regulations. This was echoed by Independent TDs Michael Lowry and Jackie Healy-Rae. Lowry claimed to have received confirmation from Fianna Fáil chief whip John Curran that Gormley would take account of the views of himself, Healy-Rae and "a number of Fianna Fáil backbenchers" in amendments to the proposed legislation. "If our concerns are addressed in these amendments we will vote for the Bill. If they are not we won't. End of story. He'd be politically wise to deal with those amendments in the spirit with which they were put forward," Lowry warned. O'Sullivan felt so strongly about the matter that he wrote to Cowen to put on the record that he had voted for the legislation to ban stag hunting despite what he believed was right. "I supported the Wildlife Amendment Bill against my better judgement, but also mindful of the fact it was part of the programme for government and had the potential of bringing down the Government." He said Fianna Fáil had "honoured our commitment" and he expected Gormley to "honour his commitment" to exempt clubs registered with the HAI from the Dog Breeding Establishments Bill. In a clear message to the Greens to stand firm on the issue, the chairwoman of the Irish Society for the Prevention of Cruelty to Animals (ISPCA), Barbara Bent, said the Bill had to be passed or an opportunity that animal welfare activists had been waiting for 30 years for would be lost.

Meanwhile a new threat to the Government's stability was issued from Donegal, when it emerged that the colourful TD for Donegal North East Dr Jim McDaid had written to Healy-Rae on Tuesday, ahead of the close Dáil vote on legislation to ban stag hunting, to say he would also oppose the Wildlife Amendment Bill. McDaid did not even oppose the contents of the Bill, but he stressed his desire for a general election to take place without delay. "It is my intention to join you, not because I oppose the Bill, but because I have been calling for a general election for over a year now," McDaid said in an email to Healy-Rae. "Should this Bill fail, the agreement between Fianna Fáil and the Greens will result in the aforementioned consequence." In the event, McDaid, who was already without the Fianna Fáil whip, backed the Government, but his threat served to further highlight the precariousness of the Coalition's majority. McDaid had been expelled from the parliamentary party when he abstained in a vote on the cervical cancer vaccination programme in November 2008. Dr Jimmy Devins and Eamon Scanlon had resigned from the parliamentary party in August 2008 after the loss of cancer services in their Sligo-North Leitrim constituency but, like McDaid, they remained party members and consistently voted with the Government. Joe Behan left Fianna Fáil and became an Independent TD over 2008 budget cuts.

Although the voting intentions of a small number of Fianna Fáil deputies remained unclear until the very last moment, the dog breeding legislation passed easily in the Dáil by 92 votes to 50, with the Labour Party this time voting with the Government.

The Welfare of Greyhounds Bill 2010 moved to restrict the number of times female dogs can be bred to six, to address concerns about bitches carrying excessive numbers of litters, and set a minimum breeding age of 15 months. Breaches of the proposed law could incur fines of up to €5,000 and a six-month prison sentence. Cowen and Gormley agreed to introduce the new codes of practice applying to the self-regulated greyhound industry by 1 January 2011. Under the new Bill, establishments with four or more bitches over 15 months that had been used, or were being used, for breeding had to be registered as breeding establishments. The operation of unregistered establishments was to be outlawed, although a grace period would apply following the enactment of legislation to allow for registration.

While a bitch could generally have no more than six litters, up to two additional litters could be bred in cases where a vet authorises this will not harm the animal, according to the legislation. Welfare officers with powers to inspect establishments would be appointed by local authorities, the Irish Greyhound Board and the Irish Coursing Club. They would be able to give direction to allow for the destruction of greyhounds in pain, distress or acute states of neglect.

The Bill also included regulations for the identification of greyhounds, as well as traceability requirements when dogs are sold. The Bill did not apply to greyhounds owned as pets but to dogs entered in the Irish Greyhound Stud Book, including those in the racing and coursing industries. Litters born to greyhounds under 15 months could not be registered and these dogs would not be permitted to race or be used at coursing events.

CHAPTER 11

GARGLEGATE AND GOLFGATE

BATTLE-WEARY FIANNA FÁIL TDs AND SENATORS GATHERED FOR their parliamentary party's annual think in at the Ardilaun Hotel in Galway in the middle of September 2010. After the tub-thumping speeches and long drawn-out workshops aimed at rallying the troops were over, there were invaluable opportunities for the party's foot soldiers to mingle with some of the normally remote officer class in a casual setting before the relentless rhythm of the Dáil term struck up once again.

Fianna Fáil politicians liked to think they knew a little more about letting their hair down than their counterparts in the Greens, and indeed they did. Dan Boyle certainly could be relied upon to whip out his guitar and get a sing-along going whenever the Greens had a weekend away, and "from time to time on a Wednesday night there'd be some gathering of us having one drink or two in the Dáil bar," he said. However, the Green gatherings were generally tame affairs by comparison to the no-holds-barred joviality of the Fianna Fáil events. Eamon Ryan enjoyed a few beers on occasion when there were no pressing engagements to attend the next morning, but John Gormley was invariably tucked up in bed before any festivities got underway.

Brian Cowen was a different kind of party leader. In the Ardilaun on the evening of 13 September, Cowen and his colleagues relaxed in their traditional fashion: by partying late into the night and well into the next morning in the comfortable hotel bar. A number of journalists mingled with the politicians, as had been the norm at such events over many years. Cowen was prevailed upon to perform a party piece and he rendered a hearty version of the ballad, 'The Lakes of Pontchartrain', to great and genuine applause. Long renowned as a skilled mimic, the Taoiseach brought the house down with his hilarious impersonations of the veteran GAA commentator Micheál Ó Muircheartaigh and a number of other popular sporting figures. He wagged his forefinger at a merry band of reporters who were looking on, jovially cautioning them to adopt a 'what goes on tour, stays on tour' approach to his performance. And then he appeared on national radio just a handful of hours after retiring, inevitably delivering a congested and halting performance with a number of verbal slip-ups. During the interview, Cowen described the Croke Park Agreement on public service pay and reform as the Good Friday Agreement, before correcting himself. He also said legislation to ban corporate donations to political parties, then being insisted upon by the Green Party, was in place, before correcting himself to say that it was being prepared.

While Cowen's Morning Ireland interview during the

previous year's think in might have featured more or less the same poor standard of tone and delivery, the mood of the country had changed so much in the 12 months that had passed since then that listeners were in no mood to accept politicians who appeared to be operating at anything but the top of their game. As Trevor Sargent assessed it: "There was a hostility there that was going to be negative pretty much anyway, but there was also a tiredness on the part of the public at listening to this lack of clarity and clichés, I suppose. When he mixed up – I mean this can happen, I know – but it was more significant because it was the Taoiseach, mixing up the Croke Park agreement with the Good Friday Agreement. One would think they're pretty obviously different."

While it was by no means the first poor media contribution from Cowen, practically the whole country was talking about the Taoiseach's particularly sub-standard performance in such an important interview slot that morning, and the internet was already alive with speculation about Cowen's condition when Fine Gael TD Simon Coveney tweeted: "God, what an uninspiring interview by Taoiseach this morning. He sounded halfway between drunk and hungover and totally disinterested … " That tweet turned out to be a game-changer. The fact that an Opposition frontbench spokesman had dared to publicly question Cowen's level of sobriety presented reporters still in the hotel, specifically TV3's Ursula Halligan, with the opportunity to legitimately doorstep the Taoiseach and ask him questions about the matter.

"Absolutely not. That's ridiculous. It's not true at all … Really, that's uncalled for," a shocked-looking Cowen protested after he was confronted.

Cowen's affronted denial inevitably bounced the story in the direction of the international media, making the already mortified leader of the country nothing a short of a laughing stock across the world. Could anything be worse at a time of such severe domestic economic crisis? The obligatory suffix indicating the incident had been elevated to the status of political scandal was swiftly attached: the episode quickly became known as "Garglegate." Shame was heaped upon ridicule when a photograph of a particularly disheveled-looking Cowen was featured on NBC's Tonight with Jay Leno programme in the United States, where the braying audience were encouraged by the presenter to decide whether Cowen was actually a bar-tender, a stand-up comedian or possibly a politician. Looking back, Boyle maintained Coveney's tweet about Cowen was a step too far. "Simon Coveney I think went over the top, you know. People talk about me and my tweeting. That was an intensely personal one and no-one seemed to give out to him about it … I think he could have said the same thing differently: 'Taoiseach less than inspiring' or something like that, rather than to make a personal comment." Boyle said he believed chronic weariness rather than the ill-effects of alcohol had caused the problems with Cowen's broadcast performance that morning. "He's not a clear speaker at the best of times anyway; he's got a particular accent. I don't think it was drink anyway; I think it was tiredness." Boyle believed Coveney, as a relative newcomer to Twitter, probably did not realise at the time the impact his tweet would have. "I think he had 14 tweets before that, and he probably hasn't tweeted much since." There was an unexpected little personal boost for Boyle, however: "Strangely enough, I got 1,000 extra Twitter followers because of him doing that!"

In the meantime, Cowen's shaken Ministers were forced to scramble to his defence. "I often have a frog in my throat in the morning," was Transport Minister Noel Dempsey's offering. The son of former taoiseach Charles Haughey, the Minister of State for Education and Skills Seán Haughey, said he understood the Taoiseach had a cold. Mary Hanafin, now serving as Minister for Tourism, Culture and Sport, blamed a "sinus issue." She said Cowen was being knocked because he was "hoarse and groggy and congested early in the morning, which does happen an awful lot of people, particularly to the first person to whom you are speaking in the morning." Defence Minister Tony Killeen went as far as to claim that the background noise in the hotel at breakfast time – "clattering knives and forks and teapots and all kinds of stuff" – could have distracted the Taoiseach. It all sounded more than a little desperate.

A humbled Cowen subsequently promised to be "a bit more cautious" about how he conducted his social life in future. Indicating however that he did not quite understand the damage to his reputation the long night in the Ardilaun had inflicted, he continued to describe it in terms of being "just a get together, a sing along with the gang in the conviviality of the company." The man who would eventually succeed Cowen as Fianna Fáil leader, the then Minister for Foreign Affairs Micheál Martin, who was a match for Gormley when it came to clean living, was clearly well able to understand fully the seriousness of what had transpired. Although he had ducked away from reporters when first questioned about Garglegate, he later intoned: "I think we have to really organise ourselves in a way that matches the mood of the people."

What would the sober Greens do now? The junior coalition partners went to Leighlinbridge, Co. Carlow, for their own think-in that very same week. There was no danger of a similar performance from Gormley, of course, and the Greens contented themselves with a low-key dinner and a moderate amount of wine. The mood was good-humoured, but quiet. "One of the rare occasions, I guess, when it helps to have a teetotal leader," an aide confided.

Gormley had been spotted with the odd glass of wine in his hand in the past, but many party workers had not witnessed their focused leader relaxing with a drink for years. The leader sounded a little strained but as fresh as ever when it came his turn to perform in the important *Morning Ireland* interview slot. Liam Reid, Gormley's press advisor, who had been listening anxiously on his headphones outside the hotel door, rushed inside to tell his boss he had done a good job. Gormley was furious, however, that the party's meticulously-planned event was dominated by questions about Cowen, although to outsiders that would have been seen as inevitable. He attempted, unsuccessfully, to close down the controversy and shift the focus onto Green-sponsored legislation, insisting that corporate donations would be banned during the lifetime of the Government and claiming a directly-elected mayor would save Dublin money in the long-term. Try as he might, however, Gormley could not divert the attention of reporters at the think in from the impact of Cowen's antics. Questions continued about the Greens opinion of Cowen's so-called "off day", and the impact it would have on relations between the Coalition partners in future. The Greens were interested in stable government, Gormley said, and he did not like "personalised politics" or political gossip. Casting aspersions about whether or not someone was "inebriated" was not helpful, he added.

Gormley revealed the matter had been discussed at Cabinet that week, after which citizens had seen Cowen apologising to the nation on television. The Taoiseach had "volunteered" to deliver the public apology and the Green Party Ministers had not asked him to do so, Gormley said. "He apologised for what had occurred, he admitted it was a 'below-par' interview and he has said that he meant no disrespect to the Irish people. I accept that. That was what I accepted when he spoke about it at Cabinet and as far as we're concerned we want to leave the matter there and to focus on the real issues which affect people in their daily lives." The whole episode was a "regrettable distraction" and all politicians had given poor interviews. "We can all have off days. We've all had the experience of giving a bad interview now and again; it's as simple as that. As far as we're concerned we want to focus on the issues at hand. I think that's what the Irish people want," he said. Still the questions continued on the same theme, and Gormley became more and more infuriated. Asked if he had confidence in Cowen as Taoiseach, Gormley said "Yes" and Dan Boyle said the Green leader was speaking for the entire party. Eamon Ryan concurred, rolling out the old mantra: "Fianna Fáil is Fianna Fáil, we're the Green Party. Let Fianna Fáil manage its own affairs."

In reality, Gormley had had enough and wanted out of Government, while Ryan held the opposite view. Since August, Gormley had harbored a deep sense of foreboding about what was coming down the tracks and how it would impact on the party. He had made his views clear to colleagues and he renewed his appeal the following month, Paul Gogarty said.

"John ear-marked around September: 'Look, it's going to get really bad guys, I think we should pull out of Government now'. We kind of said, well we've stuff to do. We've got to do the right thing and the right thing is making decisions, even if they're unpopular, and trying to get our legislation passed if we can," Gogarty said. "John was right from a political point of view. I think we would have been fucked anyway but he was right about trying to get out before that tough Budget. He'd actually come to the conclusion that we'd just got to go." Strangely for Gogarty, normally so loyal to Gormley and somewhat frosty towards Ryan, he found himself singing from the same hymn sheet as the Dublin South deputy in this instance. "Eamon would have been of a totally different view [from John] anyway, and unusually I was kind of siding with

Eamon on this one ... I still felt for the time being we had to stay in and do the right thing," he said.

Boyle was on the same page as Ryan and Gogarty, and acknowledged Gormley's growing exasperation with the situation. "John found it frustrating. He found it very frustrating. He made an argument all the time. It would have been myself and Eamon who would have argued against him." Sargent, as the previous leader of the party, had "made a conscious decision not to undermine John at any opportunity" and so kept his counsel, Boyle said. The two newish junior Ministers, Ciaran Cuffe and Mary White, were obviously also keen for the party to stay on in Government so they could attempt to make their mark. Any other political party would have fallen apart if the TDs and Senators were prepared to repeatedly attempt to countermand the leader in this way, but not the Greens. "A leader in the Green context is consensual, it's collegiate. We don't have the 'uno duce, una voce' approach," Boyle explained. Looking back with the benefit of hindsight, however, Boyle said he wished Gormley had adopted a far more traditional political approach and put his foot down once and for all. "He should have been more assertive," Boyle said with a rueful laugh.

An unfortunate pattern was emerging. At the Green's think-in in Malahide, Co. Dublin in January 2011, there was yet another fraught press conference as the Greens tried to battle their way through one more storm involving the Fianna Fáil leader which had broken in the media on the eve of their meeting. Recognising that this storm was much more serious, however, the Greens' reaction, behind the scenes at least, was a little different this time. The economic and political scene had altered so much since September 2010 that an entirely different response was required. A game of golf was at the centre of this latest controversy. The Green Party had known nothing about a golf game and dinner Cowen had enjoyed with Sean FitzPatrick, then still chairman of Anglo Irish Bank, at the Druids Glen complex in Co. Wicklow in July 2008. The episode was disclosed in a book, The FitzPatrick Tapes, by *Sunday Times* journalists Tom Lyons and Brian Carey. Fintan Drury, a friend of Cowen's who was then an Anglo director, was also present on the occasion referred to, although the Taoiseach insisted it was a social meeting and the affairs of Anglo were not discussed. This happened just months before the Government guaranteed all the deposits and bonds of the State's main financial institutions.

Sargent said the Greens had been totally in the dark about this latest controversial disclosure. "No, we didn't have any inkling of such an event. It was completely mind-blowing. It was just before our think-in, so it was that Sunday and then we were meeting on Monday and Tuesday." Even Sargent had got into Twitter by now and he tweeted breezily on Monday morning on his way to the party's two-day meeting at the Grand Hotel in Malahide. "I got this heavy response from Damian in our press office: please don't tweet because Monday is our quiet day for thinking." The media had not been invited on the Monday and there was much for the Greens to consider, so the party strategists did their best to keep their politicians out of public view that day. Discussions were naturally dominated by the fallout from what had already become known as "Golfgate" – even Gormley adopted the terminology.

Sargent said the Greens were frustrated that their event was once again overshadowed by a scandal involving their troubled Coalition partners. "It was a total shock to the system but a certain amount of déjà vu as John mentioned because when we'd been in Leighlinbridge in Carlow at the previous think-in the media scrum was completely dominated by 'Garglegate' and how where we going to respond to that," Sargent said. "So it makes for a very frustrating attempt to get across what needs to be done in Government, what you have been doing in Government and how you relate to what's happening in Government when this thing becomes a storyline as if it's from a soap opera. So there we were again dealing with an all too similar situation," he added.

Boyle said the Greens were deeply uncomfortable with both the timing and the optics of the 'Golfgate' revelations, which shook the junior Coalition partner. "It did. It didn't surprise us, but that it was still ongoing … We didn't put it down to anything sinister but again it was a cultural difference between ourselves and Fianna Fáil. That Fianna Fáil, even at that stage, wouldn't have seen that as being inappropriate; that was the disturbing aspect of it." In Malahide, Gormley, choosing his language judiciously, said the party had not uncovered any evidence of impropriety on the Taoiseach's part. Some checks had indeed been made, with

Donall Geoghegan contacting Kevin Cardiff, the secretary general of the Department of Finance, to establish definitively that no representations had been made by Cowen following the contact with FitzPatrick. Having established that this was the case, the Greens therefore said they would continue in Government, despite Cowen's failure to disclose the contact with FitzPatrick, until the important Finance Bill had completed its passage through the Oireachtas the following month. Gormley did say the contact should have been put into the public domain earlier, which was an implicit criticism of the Taoiseach, who he stopped short of endorsing at the end of the think-in. But the major part of Gormley's ineffective fury was once again reserved for expressing frustration that the second think-in meeting of his party in recent months had been overshadowed by the details of a controversy surrounding the leader of Fianna Fáil. "The last time we met as a group at the last think-in, we were talking about what's referred to now as Garglegate. Now we are talking about Golfgate. We are concentrating our efforts on that when we, a policy-driven party, want to talk about policy and we are talking about the minutiae of a golf game," Gormley fumed. The Greens' second day out at the seaside was ending badly. "We are not Sherlock Holmes. We have done what we can in the circumstances," he said. "As far as possible, we have tried to establish any impropriety and we have been unable to find any evidence."

The furore masked what was really going on behind the scenes at the think-in, however, where Gormley was finally gaining support for his long-held desire to drop everything and leave Government immediately. Some of the usual suspects countered with the by now tired old argument that the Greens could not be expected to deal with an internal Fianna Fáil matter, but Boyle said at the time the party was taking the matter "very seriously." In fact it was being taken much more seriously than any observers suspected at the time. "The process for us at that think tank ... would've been about how long are we going to stay in Government? It would've been developing our exit strategy, I guess," Boyle revealed.

Meanwhile, Opposition politicians saw their opportunity and were having a field day at the Greens expense. The then justice spokesman for Fine Gael Alan Shatter, who would be appointed Minister for Justice after the election, also described the latest revelations as serious, "extremely serious," adding that if Green Ministers were unaware of the contacts then there had been a total breakdown of trust in Government, and it was untenable that the Green Party continued in office for a further day with Fianna Fáil. Labour's then spokeswoman on finance Joan Burton, who was made Minister for Social Protection after the election, said it was "beyond belief that there was no discussion at these encounters of the rapidly deteriorating position of the bank." There was a bizarre incident at the Malahide think-in, when two Sinn Féin councillors, Dessie Ellis and Larry O'Toole, made an unsuccessful effort to enter the meeting and mount a protest calling for an immediate election. The unhappy pair managed to get lost in the corridors of the Grand Hotel, until some reporters pointed them in the direction of the Marconi Suite, where press officer Damian Connon stood with his arms folded across his chest, doing a convincing turn as a bouncer. With impeccable manners, Connon borrowed the words of the early nineties hit single to politely inform Ellis and O'Toole: "your name's not down; you're not coming in."

A striking fact to note is that when assessing Cowen's contribution in retrospect, Green Party personnel are often much kinder to the now former Fianna Fáil leader than his own party people were towards the end of his time in power and subsequently. "Decent" is probably the most common word to describe Cowen employed by Greens. Gormley obviously spent more time with Cowen than any other Green. Gormley and Ryan would meet before Cabinet early on Tuesday mornings and then Gormley would meet Cowen and the pair of leaders would run through the upcoming agenda, anticipating sticking points and trying to explain the finer points of their respective party's positions in terms the other could easily understand. "It ended up where probably I was as close to him as any of his Fianna Fáil people. It's an unusual thing. We always actually had a good, I think fairly good, relationship. I think he was a decent guy," Gormley said. While Cowen's watchword was loyalty, he eventually disappointed and alienated even his closest supporters. Gormley believed the Taoiseach had previously been put on a pedestal that was too high for a mortal politician, describing Cowen as "a guy who was seen as the brightest politician in Ireland at one stage." It is true that Cowen was portrayed as a shining star in the Irish political firmament for a period before he became Taoiseach. "The media were lionising the guy," Gormley insisted. "So he was never quite as good as they made him out to be, but he was never as bad as they made him out to be either," he said. "He was dealing with a whole series of issues, as we all were, but the only thing, if I was going to be critical of him, is he still had a belief in the old paradigm. He still believed that if we could just get a few houses built everything would be grand, and of course that just wasn't on anymore. That was just gone." But still, something like fondness remained: "I get on well with him; I don't hold any grudges at all."

Gogarty said Cowen's first loyalty was to the Fianna Fáil party, but that did not make him disloyal to the country, and the good he did should be recognized in retrospect. "I feel really sorry for Brian Cowen, I really do, on a human level ... Brian Cowen obviously made mistakes. The Greens made loads of mistakes. I made loads of mistakes. But I think Brian Cowen is a decent man who has the country's interests at heart," Gogarty said. "I empathise with Brian Cowen." Asked about Cowen, Geoghegan said: "Believe it nor not, I like him", while Boyle was less kind: "It was an open secret that he didn't want us in the first place," he said. Sargent likened Cowen's almost tragic descent, from a rising bright intellectual light to a greatly diminished and almost paralysed presence, to the change that overcame Michael Noonan when he took charge of Fine Gael for a brief period in 2001 and 2002. "Something similar happened to Michael Noonan when he became leader. He went from being the witty, acerbic, confident character who could take on all comers and people were rallying to him, felt comfortable with him, had confidence in him and he just froze as leader," Sargent said. "Unfortunately Brian Cowen I think had probably fallen into a similar problem; sadly for him and sadly for the country," he added.

Meanwhile, the Government's feeble response to a report into clerical child sex abuse that rocked the country left much to be desired and the Coalition which the Greens were party to once again appeared to be out of touch with the shocked indignation of the public mood at the time. Judge Yvonne Murphy had been appointed to lead a commission of investigation set up by the government to inquire into the handling of clerical child sex abuse allegations in the Dublin archdiocese between 1975 and 2004. The Murphy commission had written to the Vatican's Congregation for the Doctrine of the Faith seeking information on reports sent to it by Dublin archdiocese and received no reply. The commission then wrote to the papal nuncio in Dublin asking that he forward to it all documents in his possession which might be relevant. Again, no reply came back.

When the Murphy report was published at the end of 2009, it found that four successive archbishops of the Dublin Catholic archdiocese had handled allegations of child sexual abuse with "denial, arrogance and cover-up." The structures and rules of the Catholic Church had facilitated the cover-up of abuse, the report also said. Giving what was deemed to be the Government's official response to the report, Cowen described as a "crushing verdict" the finding that the standing of the Church as an institution was placed above the basic safety of children. However, he said it was up to religious organisations and their members to determine the appropriateness of various individuals to hold ecclesiastical office. Cowen concluded with his view that both the Vatican and the commission "acted in good faith in this matter, even if the best outcome was not achieved."

Even the elements appeared to be against this most unlucky of Governments, and the so-called climate change experts in the Green Party took the lion's share of public criticism. Severe flooding at the beginning of 2008 and the end of 2009 was followed by heavy snowfall and sub-zero temperatures which created treacherous conditions and brought the country to a standstill at the start of 2010 and once again in 2011, when Gormley bridled at being dubbed "the Minister for Snow" by RTÉ presenter Miriam O'Callaghan in a television interview conducted when Dempsey was on holiday in Malta. Supplies of grit and salt ran low and water restrictions affected many areas including Gormley's Dublin South-East constituency, where his constituents would find it hard to forgive their local TD and Minister for the Environment. The controversy over the incinerator rumbled on, meanwhile, with Gormley facing criticism over his handling of the planned Poolbeg facility in Dublin's docklands. All TDs in the constituency appeared to oppose the project, with some accusing them of adopting a 'not in my back yard' approach, but only one of the deputies was Minister for the Environment. Gormley was on a collision course with the four Dublin local authorities and the project's promoters. Ryan's Energy, Communications and Natural Resources portfolio proved less contentious, but progress appeared to be glacial and positive press coverage proved hard to come by as the State's financial position continued to deteriorate.

CHAPTER 12

THREE LITTLE LETTERS – IMF

THE GOVERNOR OF THE CENTRAL BANK PROFESSOR PATRICK Honohan took to the airwaves on the morning of Thursday, November 18, 2010, to confirm that Ireland would be receiving substantial financial assistance from the International Monetary Fund (IMF). The loan package would be in the region of "tens of billions", he revealed to anxious listeners whose Government had been attempting to keep them in a state of ignorance.

Eamon Ryan was forced to make an immediate, live response because he was standing by in the studio from where RTÉ Radio One's *Morning Ireland* programme was broadcast. He had turned up at the Montrose headquarters in time to catch the 8 am headlines, believing he was going to go on air straight after the 'It Says In The Papers' slot, which was particularly gloomy that day, until the broadcast team informed him otherwise. "They said, 'Hold on a second, we've got Patrick Honohan on first.'" Honohan had called in from Frankfurt, where he was attending the European Central Bank's governing council meeting. "I said, 'Fine' and listened to what he had to say and then I had to make a response," Ryan said.

Ryan admitted that the Greens had gone to ground the previous Friday, when the financial newswire Bloomberg broke a story claiming that Ireland was being urged to become the second euro zone country, after Greece, to avail of emergency aid in order to contain the debt crisis. Recalling that weekend later, he said: "Certainly on the Friday morning I would have got a call from Bloomberg, [saying] 'We hear you're going into a facility,' I said 'Who'd you hear it from?' ... This is coming from Berlin and Brussels. I hope I'm not breaching their sources but basically it was coming from a high level and that was really difficult," Ryan said. He immediately began to make urgent calls to Finance Minister Brian Lenihan and Department of Finance officials, as well as to his own party colleagues. "My sense was that there were talks starting to happen but there was nothing certain. There was no way that it was a done deal," he said. "Over that weekend ... my sense of it was we don't know where this is going, we have to be careful because it's not clear." So the senior Greens kept schtum and advised their party colleagues to do the same, as Gormley also confirmed: "Eamon had heard that some discussions had taken place so we thought it wiser not to say anything in public until we had confirmation."

The Fianna Fáil Ministers who had committed to public appearances in the days that followed found it more difficult to hide behind a discreet cloak of silence, however. Dermot Ahern and Noel Dempsey signed their own political death warrants in a spectacular fashion with a Laurel and Hardy-style appearance on the television evening news when asked about the possibility of a bailout on Monday while attending an event. "I'm not aware of it, nor is Noel," Ahern said, as his colleague shook his bowed head and pursed his lips. It was all "fiction" and "speculation," Ahern had told presenter Sean O'Rourke on The Week in Politics programme the night before. By this stage, Ryan said, Fianna Fáil and the Greens were no longer even attempting to co-ordinate media appearances. "I don't know how they were caught in that way in terms of the communications," Ryan said. "I think it was very unfortunate [for] Noel Dempsey and Dermot Ahern ... because it was one of those instances ... where you go out and you say something and it doesn't look good for you personally." The sound bites and images that were snipped from the Fianna Fáil Ministers responses to reporters' questions about the possibility of a rescue package "really lost the public confidence" and "did huge damage" when the facts finally emerged the following week, Ryan said.

Clarity had been provided initially by Honohan, after many days of confusion when the country was under intense international scrutiny, and during which time Ministers continued to play down the likelihood of a bailout after the Cabinet had formally decided to begin discussions with the IMF and EU. A schedule of Cabinet records released to *The Irish Times'* chief reporter Carl O'Brien in April 2011 revealed that a memorandum regarding the "Minister for Finance's engagement with the IMF, European Central Bank (ECB) and European Commission" was discussed by some members of Cabinet at least on Tuesday, November 16. Ryan was later interested to read the analysis of Morgan Kelly, professor of economics at University College Dublin, who claimed on 7 May 2011 in *The Irish Times* that: "Rarely has a finance minister been so deftly sliced off at the ankles by his central bank governor." Ryan's understanding of Kelly's analysis was that a strategy of denial and an attempt to play hardball in order to strengthen the State's negotiating position "worked until, I suppose, the Central Bank governor Patrick Honohan came out and said, 'Oh, we are going in' on *Morning Ireland*."

Not for the first time, Gormley wanted the party he led to get out of Government immediately. "My view was that it would have been better to leave Government at that point rather than going through with the worst budget in the history of the State. The combination of the IMF coming in here and the Budget could only result in electoral meltdown," Gormley said. Since August, he had been desperately attempting to bring the other members of the parliamentary party around to his point of view. "I knew there was something stirring. I knew from that summer that there was a real chance. I said to my guys a few times, 'We can't be in Government when the IMF comes in here because it would be a disaster', but I said, 'They are coming in guys: make no mistake.'" Gormley said he also tried to make headway with some of the Fianna Fáil Ministers. Like some other Greens, he felt the Fianna Fáil Ministers had been kept in the dark about the seriousness of the situation, but he was dismissed as "a Jonah", a jinxed character whose presence brought misfortune on his colleagues. He attempted to bring the matter up with colleagues quite a number of times, he said. "Anytime I would say to Lenihan at Cabinet, I said it a few times at Cabinet, Lenihan would say, 'John, John we're funded until July. We're funded up 'til then.' He repeated the line that we were funded up to the summer. And if you pursued the matter you were seen as a type of Jonah anyway," Gormley said.

"Brian Lenihan and Brian Cowen did not inform the Cabinet members. Brian Cowen told me that he had told [European Commission chief José Manuel] Barosso that he knew nothing about the IMF coming in here," he added. And yet, in retrospect, Gormley had some sympathy for the position that Cowen and Lenihan found themselves in. "The problem was that in the financial world you cannot say that there's even a chance of the IMF coming in because it becomes a self-fulfilling prophecy at that stage," he conceded. And also, to have spoken the words out loud would have damaged Ireland's negotiating position when it came to striking a deal. Gormley said that after Honohan's clear and direct intervention, Lenihan was seen as having lost credibility with the public, "because he was seen as being mendacious, and Honohan was presented as the truth teller." Gormley insisted that was not an accurate portrayal of Lenihan, however. "Those are caricatures; they don't bear out the reality."

Meanwhile, Gormley was doing all he could to persuade his

parliamentary colleagues that the game was up for the Greens in Government, but his pleas continued to fall on deaf ears. "I think the cleanest of all would have been about the time of the IMF and just said, 'Bye bye. It's over. Clean break. We're gone.' That would have been simple, clean, but my colleagues said, 'No, we have to do the right thing by the country.'" Gormley, possibly as a result of his natural pessimism, was way ahead of the rest of the Greens when it came to understanding that the IMF delegation was approaching Irish shores. Assessing Gormley's leadership throughout this period, Trevor Sargent said: "John is capable of depths of despair alright, but he's also capable of great incisive and intuitive determination. When others don't see how things are panning out John will call it and people will appreciate that somebody has called it, because it wasn't going to be called otherwise."

The Greens had been hearing about the possibility of the IMF's arrival for quite some time, with Gormley getting strong hints from Germany through contacts forged during his stint at the University of Freiburg in the 1980s, where he cemented his devotion to Green politics. Naturally, he was communicating what he was hearing to close parliamentary colleagues, such as Sargent. "I remember John had heard, because he is a German teacher and German speaker, he'd heard from Germany that there was talk of the IMF coming in here. And when he put it to Brian Cowen the response was, 'Well they're just trying to bounce us into the IMF and it's scare tactics to undermine us and weaken our position and make us appear worse than we are.' So that was the retort."

Cowen's response seemed plausible at the time, Sargent said. "That was the kind of response which dampened down the awareness, if you like, of how serious things were. And then of course the whole thing blew up." Ajai Chopra, the deputy director of the IMF's European department, would shortly be photographed passing a beggar as he walked from Merrion Row towards the Central Bank in an iconic image that was flashed around the world. "Since then of course, with the power of hindsight, I've spoken to people in financial services as far away as Hong Kong and they knew the IMF was coming in and they didn't believe a word coming out of Merrion Street," Sargent said. "It just highlighted how dysfunctional and how panicked our own Department of Finance was, that they were in a state of delusion effectively and couldn't even tell their Minister what was happening because they didn't want to face up to it themselves. So the mixed messages and the lack of communication went quite deep in the system. The whole psyche of the system was in shock."

Ryan too acknowledged that Gormley had repeatedly told party colleagues the arrival of the IMF was a possibility. "When people were going, 'Oh no, the IMF won't come in', he would in fairness to him be saying. 'This is a real prospect.'" The crystallisation of the Greek debt crisis over the summer, combined with worsening figures from Anglo Irish Bank, finally brought the reality home to other Greens. "That was only really when we started to think about it significantly. And I think roughly at that time internally my sense – if you ask a family what happened you'll get five different stories, six different stories depending on how many in the family – but my sense around that summer when the Greek debt crisis came and after the Anglo figures started to get worse than expected, I think we were starting to say then and sense internally we needed a change of Government." The Greens were reading and being influenced by the commentary of respected analysts such as the late former taoiseach Dr Garret FitzGerald and *The Irish Times'* political editor Stephen Collins. The Greens interpretation of what they were recommending was that the Government needed to complete the budgetary process in December and have an election in 2011. "I think internally that would have been our fairly commonly held position ... and not a clever thing politically in some ways because if you're clever politically you don't do tough Budgets, you cut and run, but we had a genuine sense ... that this Government needs to put through a difficult but necessary Budget to get us out of economic difficulties," Ryan said. "And I think in the back of our minds there wasn't a certainty, there wasn't a sense that the IMF are definitely going to come in, but it was certainly something we were considering from the summer onwards as a possibility."

And it became a real prospect even for the ultra-optimistic Ryan when in November 2010 German Chancellor Angela Merkel pushed for private investors to share the burden of the euro debt crisis, and her remarks sent Irish borrowing costs to record levels. While Ryan did not disagree with Merkel's assessment that it was unfair for taxpayers alone to be saddled with the cost of sovereign rescues, he said her statement was "hugely damaging" for Ireland. "It was the timing of it at a time when confidence was weak after the debt crisis. It was effectively saying to the market, 'Don't go near any of these countries', and that had an immediate effect." Even then, however, he thought 2010 would not be the year in which the IMF came to Ireland. "No-one expected it to be a possibility until the following year, the next year, because we had €20 billion in cash and it's not usual for countries who have €20 billion in cash to be forced into a facility, and we were just about to engage in a four year budgetary plan which had been agreed by Brussels. So it wasn't as if we were without a strategy."

Boyle said the Greens had ignored their own leader's ominous warnings about the IMF's arrival and were taken by surprise as a consequence. "We all believed that a decision was likely in January rather than the November before that, so that caught us by surprise. And I think it caught everyone by surprise," he said. Once again, Boyle sided with Ryan against Gormley in private meetings. "John wanted to go a lot earlier. I mean, that's an open secret at this stage. He had a sense of foreboding about the whole thing and he felt the IMF was inevitable. Myself and Eamon felt that the strategy could work if given an opportunity," he said. "I must admit he [John] was convinced the IMF was coming in; myself and Eamon thought it was still a possibility. We were more optimistic. We believed the strategy could have worked." The differences in approach reflect the personality differences within the party. "John is more inclined to a negative reading of things but, that said, his political instinct is better than anyone else in the party."

Some efforts to reach out to Opposition parties and perhaps co-ordinate some type of consensus approach had taken place the previous month on foot of a Green initiative. "We had a strong sense that we needed to get in other parties because that sense of the crisis being very real became very apparent," Ryan said. Cowen took some convincing, especially after Gormley blundered by blurting out a reference to a "national government" in the course of a rather rushed interview with Today FM. Such a concept was an anathema to a Fianna Fáil leader. "It was asking Brian Cowen to take a political risk in terms of stepping out of a very typical, more traditional Fianna Fáil approach," Ryan recalled. "I don't think there's been a single instance in the history of the State where Fianna Fáil and Fine Gael have joined sides on a council not to mention in the Oireachtas, but he did it in fairness to him."

However, the traditional dynamic between Government and Opposition had changed by this stage, for a rather curious reason. The failed heave against Fine Gael leader Enda Kenny in June had propelled Michael Noonan back to the forefront of Fine Gael. Except for a stint at the head of the Dáil's powerful Public Accounts Committee, Noonan had been wandering in the political wilderness after the 2002 General Election. His brief stint as leader of Fine Gael had been disastrous and the party lost 23 seats in the General Election that year and saw its strength in

Dublin drop from 12 to three TDs. Come summer 2010, Kenny had appointed his predecessor as leader to the coveted position of finance spokesman. The position had previously been held by the man who challenged Kenny for the leadership and lost: Richard Bruton. "The change that occurred after the Enda heave had a certain effect in terms of, I don't think Richard Bruton and Brian Lenihan had a particularly close contact. I don't think Joan Burton and Brian Lenihan had [a] particularly close 'common thoughts' approach. I know that Brian Lenihan and Michael Noonan had fairly strong communications," Ryan said.

Ryan stayed in the background during this process but was involved to some extent in trying to set up the meeting of party leaders through his close contact with Fine Gael's Simon Coveney. The pair used to meet up and escape the oppressive atmosphere of Leinster House by taking regular jaunts around one of Dublin's most famous Georgian areas to clear their heads. The tall, slim, striding duo talked through various strategies that might result in bringing the leaders of the Civil War party leaders together. "We used to go out walking around Merrion Square. I'd meet him at the gate and we'd go and do a few laps of Merrion Square, just talking through, 'OK, how are we going to do this?' So I was fairly involved in it just in a background way of trying to set it up." One of Coveney's earliest tweets showed his particular attachment to this elegant city centre square with a pleasant park at its centre, although there was no mention of his Green walking partner: "Walked through magnificent Merrion Square in early morning sunshine, man writing poetry sitting on a bench, what a lift for the soul before work." Coveney had marked Ryan as his party's communications, energy and natural resources spokesman until the failed heave in which he supported Bruton, when he was shifted to transport, and after the General Election the Corkman would become Minister for Agriculture.

After some difficulty, the meeting between the party leaders was eventually set up and scheduled for 20 October 2010. It lasted for around two hours, but the occasion was not a success. The Greens had hoped for some sort of common approach on the Budget in return for a commitment to a general election in the New Year. However, it soon became clear that the Green's dream was "dead in the water," Ryan said. "Maybe that was the time we should've pulled out of Government. The inability to get the wider political system in; it would have been better to have an election and get an electoral mandate," he said in retrospect. He was convinced otherwise at the time, however. "There was the argument you're facing into the Budget that you have to do. How would you have an election and get a Budget done quickly enough?" After a huge number of painstakingly-detailed Cabinet meetings, the Government's four year budgetary plan was almost ready for submission to Brussels. Meanwhile, the European Commissioner for economic and monetary affairs Olli Rehn was on his way to Dublin to meet both Government and Opposition personnel. He was saying it was essential for Ireland to pass its Budget, and when Rehn spoke, others listened. Ryan recalled Rehn's parting words were that Ireland was going to be "at the top of the agenda" at the G20 meeting in Seoul. Ryan was confident that the Budget would pass through the Dáil. "The banking situation remained a serious problem, but at least we've taken the hard measures in terms of Nama and the assets and we have cash in hand. We [are] not in the position for an immediate bailout," he thought.

"The difficulty was at that Seoul G20 meeting. This is where world economic policy is now decided. There was a real concern, I would imagine, around Spanish banks at the time and [a] contagion effect from Ireland into Spain," he said. The Americans were particularly concerned, after a few years of terrible economic pain. "No-one should underestimate the scale of the crisis in 2008," Ryan said. Unprecedented in the lifetime of working politicians, "it looked like the Western capitalism was about to come down." Ryan's assessment was that a high-level decision taken at Seoul was what sealed Ireland's fate. "I think there was a decision made there. I'm only going from listening from a distance, we don't have membership there. There was a decision made at a very high level that something has to be done to Ireland. They have to be brought into a facility. And I think they then went away from that meeting with instructions to their civil servants or to the ECB."

Ryan said he thought Honohan must have come under huge pressure from colleagues in the ECB. "I think they felt very exposed by the level of liquidity that they'd had to put into the Irish banks. They saw money going out of the Irish banks and the need for immediate action ... they felt you needed immediate entry into the facility to be able to stop that whole process of the money going out. And I would imagine Patrick Honohan as Governor of the Central Bank, he's independent; he's got his instincts in terms of protecting the banking system and so on, and made his comments on that basis." In September the following year, 2011, Honohan said he did not regret his decision to go on radio and confirm a bailout package was being prepared. Boyle too fingered the G20 meeting in Seoul as creating the main difficulty for Ireland. "It really was German nervousness at the G20 summit in Seoul. It was just a whole series of leaks and counter leaks," Boyle said.

On Monday November 15, Brian Cowen had insisted Ireland was not making an application for EU or IMF funding for the State because the country was already funded right up to the middle of the following year. The next Sunday night Cowen and Lenihan finally confirmed the Government had formally applied for a multibillion-euro rescue package from the EU and the IMF. Sovereignty was lost and control of the country's economic affairs was no longer in the control of politicians elected by Irish voters. Ireland's humiliation was complete.

At the conclusion of a five-hour meeting that day when the Government formally decided to apply for a bailout, Gormley was asked to participate in the press event along with Cowen and Lenihan but he declined. Government Ministers had been meeting all weekend. On the Saturday, Gormley absented himself from a gathering in the Sycamore Room in Government Buildings. It was the wood-panelled room where Cowen had invited political correspondents for a briefing the previous May during one of his aborted spurts of engagement with the media. The day before he had delivered a long speech at Dublin City University in which conceded the economic and banking crisis had been made worse by domestic factors, including mistakes by Government. Gossiping about Gormley's absence, Fianna Fáil Ministers whispered that the Green leader had to be taken home "because he couldn't stick the pressure." Gormley was in constant contact with his party colleagues, however, who effectively put in a four-hour parliamentary party meeting through a series of conference calls, and they would meet again after the Cabinet meeting on Sunday. They were attempting to plan their next move as confusion swirled around.

Paul Gogarty, who contributed to the conference calls from the Iveagh Gardens, where he had brought his children to play with their cousins, complained that the Greens had been "lied to, or certainly weren't given the truth" by Fianna Fáil. Donall Geoghegan said "quite obviously there were different degrees of knowledge about what was going on within Government." Boyle's view was that everyone in Government, "with the possible exception of Brian Cowen and Brian Lenihan, were very much in the dark about everything." Ryan recalled the sense of uncertainty and helplessness: "That weekend was really tough. I mean it was the hardest, hardest, hardest time. It was hard for everyone: I remember people protesting outside the Dáil gates."

There was much talk at that time of civil unrest. There were ugly scuffles with gardai at the gates of Leinster House during a rally, with protesters attempting to gain access to the parliament complex. The ornate wrought iron gates had to be shut, creating a visual sense of disconnect between the privileged world of the Oireachtas and the increasingly difficult lives of people outside. The Green's newest Senator Mark Dearey told his terrified party colleagues that he had met a young man who told him, with utter seriousness, that it "would only take a couple of hundred people to storm the place and sort it out." Gogarty said a "massive street protest" was planned the following Saturday, the 27. "We kind of felt, Jesus Christ, this is going to blow up. The talk about a bailout is much more psychologically damaging than the actual bailout process, and all it would take would be a couple of Eirigi or Socialist Worker people to antagonise the police to do something stupid; to cause massive civil disorder and riots and loss of life possibly," Gogarty said. As Greece had battled a debt crisis with stringent austerity measures, rampaging rioters had taken to the streets. The Greens felt the passivity and reluctance to protest of the Irish people could no longer be taken for granted. "We'd seen what had happened in Greece, and although we're a little bit more sedate here in Ireland, as a group of TDs and Senators we kind of thought well Jesus if this is happening in Greece now, if something isn't done this is going to happen in Ireland," Gogarty said.

A clear indication of how loathed the Greens had become arrived when Mary White was spat on in the street in her constituency around this time. When she was crossing the road from her constituency office in Dublin Street, Carlow to get a cup of coffee she passed a well-dressed, middle-aged man. He did not speak, "but just turned round and spat on me," she said. "It was horrible; it was worse than a physical blow. You got over it of course, but that moment you had a gobbet of spit on you. And for this guy to actually do that, a man I didn't know, but [who] was obviously repulsed by the Greens in Government. It was a bit of a personal shock, that," she added. There had been other assaults on her person and property in the past, "but the spit was actually the worst because it was almost biblical: they spat at you as you went by. It was an appalling gesture. I knew we'd have a very difficult election." When White related this anecdote to her party colleagues they could barely believe the party had sunk so low in people's estimation that fury would be vented in this way. Geoghegan too recalled the mounting fear of civil disorder. "There were marches; there was danger. If you read the papers, if you heard the conversations ... the abuse people were getting," he said. "There was an attack at the Department of Finance offices. There was a lot of that going on and at the time we really did fear civil unrest."

The Greens would soon lose another man overboard when one of the party's bright young hopefuls, Gary Fitzgerald, became the latest member to resign from the party expressing disillusionment. Fitzgerald had made a formal complaint to gardaí in February, alleging Willie O'Dea had perjured himself in an affidavit in the libel case involving Maurice Quinlivan. Gardaí began an investigation which resulted in a decision by the DPP that O'Dea had no case to answer. Fitzgerald, who had been chairman of the National Executive Council, said his decision to leave the Greens was motivated by his strong objections to the terms of the EU-IMF bailout deal. "It's a recipe for a disorderly national default on our sovereign debt with all the dreadful consequences that will follow from that," he warned.

Meanwhile, domestic politics had been somehow trundling on. For some time, the Greens had been failing to persuade their Fianna Fáil colleagues to hold the Donegal South-West byelection. The TD had been without a constituency since Pat 'the Cope' Gallagher was elected to the European Parliament for Fianna Fáil in June of the previous year. Gormley and Boyle were both sons of Donegal men, with Gormley's father a school contemporary of the esteemed playwright Brian Friel, and so the pair had a particular attachment to the neglected region. On November 3, the Government was finally forced to hold a byelection on November 25, after Sinn Féin's Pearse Doherty took a High Court action to encourage the required moving of the writ. "That was extremely embarrassing to us," Boyle recalled. "We thought it was stupid on Fianna Fáil's part to keep delaying." Ironically, it was perhaps the one constituency in which Fianna Fáil could have won a byelection "if they did it early," Boyle said. "They just went into this siege mentality ... I think Brian Cowen had this fear – which is ironic given the eventual circumstances – of this death by a thousand cuts scenario." Doherty won the byelection, of course, beating off challengers Barry O'Neill of Fine Gael and Fianna Fáil's Brian O'Domhnaill.

CHAPTER 13

LEAVING, YET STAYING

THE ARRIVAL OF THE IMF ESSENTIALLY MEANT "CURTAINS" FOR the Programme for Government, and signalled that the time had finally arrived for the Greens to leave the Coalition, Trevor Sargent said. Expanding on the suggestive image about the Greens' ongoing participation in the Fianna Fáil-led administration, he said: "It was like three in a bed then. There was Fianna Fáil, the Greens … and the IMF."

The Government's mandate had been wiped out by the IMF's arrival, Sargent said. "From our point of view we really felt: This is it. The Government has lost its mandate. A Government that allows the IMF to come in on its watch can't simply carry on without any consequences." At the Greens' weekend meetings, they had agreed the current Coalition arrangement was no longer viable and therefore an election had to take place soon. The party's senior Ministers had obviously been working on their poker faces, having sat through a Cabinet meeting on the Sunday without dropping as much as a hint of what they were at that stage strongly considering, if not already agreed on in principle. The Greens had gone into conclave once again after the Cabinet meeting concluded. They reached a decision on the Sunday night, then slept on it and anxiously double-checked with each other in the morning. Were they really ready to press the self-destruct button?

It was at last time to make an announcement, and so a text message was dispatched to political correspondents on Monday morning, 22 November, 2010, landing at 11.11 am. "John Gormley will hold press conference at 11.30 am in AV Room, Leinster House," it said. After receiving the alert, members of the Dáil press corps scrambled towards the audio visual room, just off the portico leading into LH2000, while temporary accreditation was hurriedly organised for those who did not have regular access to the complex. A serious chink in the choreography emerged, however, when it proved not quite so easy to get the attention of Brian Cowen. Gormley had planned to inform the Taoiseach directly of his explosive intentions shortly after 11 am that morning. The thinking was that this would offer Cowen the courtesy of hearing the news first, without giving him enough time to actually do anything about it. The problem was that Cowen was not answering his mobile phone, however. Try as he might, Gormley could not get through on the 10-digit number known only to an elite few. It turned out Cowen was live on air at the time, doing an extended interview with his local radio station. As the minutes ticked away, and Cowen continued talking at length at the good people of counties Laois and Offaly, the Greens were facing the unsavory possibility of announcing their intentions to the waiting representatives of the national media before briefing the leader of their coalition partner. That would have been bad form in the extreme.

Finally, just as the press conference was scheduled to get underway at 11.30 am, Gormley made contact with Cowen and blurted out what he had to say. The gist of the brief and mostly one-sided conversation was that the Greens would stay in Government only until certain key financial measures were put in place, according to Sargent. "We had to wait for the Taoiseach to come off his Midland radio interview and tell him that but for the good of the country we'd be gone, but we're going as soon as these things are in place," he said. How did Cowen take the news? A master of understatement, Gormley said the Fianna Fáil leader had expressed "a certain disappointment." Brian Lenihan was also clearly unaware of what the junior Coalition partners were up to when he was door-stepped by reporters that morning. The parties were working well together in Government, he insisted. Were the Greens actually going to manage to wrong-foot the vastly more experienced Fianna Fáil? Now that truly would be a turn-up for the books.

At the press conference, Gormley's message appeared to be that the Greens would pull out of Government if Cowen refused to call an election. "We believe it is time to fix a date for a general election in the second half of January 2011," he said. However, the party would not breach what it considered to be its duty of care to the electorate by leaving power before three things were delivered: a credible four-year plan for the economy, the delivery of the Budget and the securing of funding support from the EU and IMF. There was no mention of key Green-sponsored legislation. So, it seemed, the Greens were leaving Government, but they were also staying.

Gormley told the press conference there had been "major disquiet" in the party he led over the arrival of the IMF. While he respected the constitutional prerogative of the Taoiseach to name a date for the General Election, he was also conscious of the Green Party's need to "respect ourselves and our members." It was practically an admission that the party had been operating without self respect in more recent times. Asked if the Greens had been misled by Fianna Fáil on the IMF issue, he said: "I believe that there was bad communication. We were given an official line, both Eamon Ryan and myself, which was essentially a mixed message." Gormley said the pair had been told that discussions, rather than negotiations, were taking place, and he complained about receiving "somewhat Jesuitical" answers to straightforward questions. "Under the circumstances, because of the vagueness of that particular message, we felt it a better and probably much wiser approach not to say anything. I think that approach was better under the circumstances," he said.

A junior visitor to Leinster House caused a flurry of excitement and chatter that day, as Paul Gogarty had dashed in from Lucan with his little daughter Daisy in her pushchair. The curly-haired toddler sat on her father's knee and her large teddy bear was propped atop the desk behind which the grim-faced Greens lined-up to face the media. Brightly-dressed Daisy, whether yawning or playing with her father's smartphone, was a natural magnet for the photographers' attentions. Gogarty had considered leaving his daughter in the care of someone outside the room where the press conference was taking place, but did not have time to organise anything and was also worried she might become upset in his absence. The appropriateness or otherwise of Daisy's presence in such stressful, grown-up environment sparked a mini-controversy on Joe Duffy's *Liveline* programme. "That was a terrible mistake but look, we were thinking about Ireland and the Eurozone; childcare I'm afraid wasn't top of the agenda. Perception and optics I guess probably wasn't really what was on our mind," Sargent said. "What we wanted to ensure was that we were all united: baby and all." The stress of recent days had clearly taken a visible toll on the party's newest parliamentarians, Senators Mark Dearey and Niall Ó Brolcháin, whose dazed and worried expressions resembled those normally worn by people in the deep stages of grief. Even Sargent did not appear his normal, composed self.

After Gormley had dropped the bombshell on behalf of the Greens, all those caught up inside the Leinster House bubble held their breath. A few bewildered Fianna Fáil backbenchers milled around the Leinster House portico, unable to comprehend, not for the first time, the Green Party's thinking. Some were even laughing in disbelief. Many anticipated that Cowen would go straight to the Áras and an election would be announced: the unwritten rules of politics appeared to dictate that was the only course of action open to the under-pressure Taoiseach. But he stubbornly refused to do what was expected of him, and Ryan believed he made the right choice. "Brian Cowen had a decision to make: does he go to the Park or does he agree to it? And Brian Cowen in my mind made the correct call in saying we're not going to go to the Park; we're going to get the Budget through," he said. The advice of the EU economic affairs commissioner was ringing in Ryan's ears, and was probably also fresh in Cowen's mind: "Ollie Rehn was very clear in saying you cannot do an election and a Budget at the same time." So Cowen rolled with the punch that had been delivered by the Greens and stayed put, calling an evening press conference in Government Buildings which was attended by a large contingent of international media, struggling to keep up with the rapidly changing events of that day.

Asked if he felt betrayed by the surprise move from the Greens, who had sat mute at Cabinet the day before their shock announcement, Cowen memorably said: "That is not a word that is in my lexicon at all." He bizarrely insisted he had the confidence of the Green Party. However, he did commit to allowing a general election to take place early in the New Year, with the Budget to be passed before then. There would be a time for political accountability by the electorate, he said. It was quite incredible that the show was kept on the road for another while given the lack of trust between Fianna Fáil and the Greens at this stage, but Ryan acknowledged that the Coalition partners were bound together by a set of circumstances that were utterly unprecedented in Irish politics. "In any other circumstances that Government would have broken up that day, but it was just the circumstance we were in that we were both compelled to get a Budget through, because that was part of keeping the country together." Increasing the sense of fragility, a number of Fianna Fáil backbenchers called publicly on Cowen to resign and two Independents who backed the Government, Michael Lowry and Jackie Healy-Rae, withdrew their support.

Meanwhile, confusion started to bubble up around what the Green Party's message, delivered that morning, had actually been. The perhaps clumsily-worded statement was instantly interpreted in the obvious way: as meaning the party was calling for an election some time between 15 and 31 January. But some Greens later claimed they were not in fact fixated on that particular period and simply wanted to ensure that an announcement about an impending election would be made during that time. It was now the Green Party's turn to become Jesuitical, it seemed. Ryan admitted more care should have been taken to ensure the clarity of the words used in order to avoid subsequent confusion. "Just to cap it all off, the wording was done really quickly. So, lessons learned, you take your time on certain things. The line I think used was the election would be called by January, and you can interpret that two ways," he said.

Sargent also claimed the speed with which the event was pulled together resulted in misinterpretation. "It was so hastily arranged that I think there was a bit of confusion when John said January," he said. "It's not his [Gormley's] call when to have the election. He wanted it called in January because we didn't want to delay the election one day beyond what was necessary for the country to have a level of stability that would allow us to have an election." Boyle said he was to blame for the misunderstanding of what was actually intended by the words he had suggested. He felt there was a subtle distinction between the two possible propositions. "It was far too subtle … it was my formulation, so it was my fault," he said. "Our strategy had been misunderstood anyway because we knew that leaving directly in November would've caused such ructions in the markets that it would've been irresponsible to leave Government then. So we said we would stay – pass the Finance Bill, pass the Budget – which we thought was responsible. And then we said that we would foresee an election being called in January."

Such an interpretation might have made sense to the Greens, but it made little or no sense to almost everyone else. Gormley subsequently admitted the concept of leaving but staying was too complex for most observers to understand, and even those who might have thought it was the right thing to do still did not show their appreciation for it when the time of reckoning came. "There's no room for complexity in politics, none, and that's just the terrible reality. The idea that we're leaving Government but first of all we're going to go through with the Budget?" Gormley said. "I mean, not one person thanked us on the doorstep for it. Not one person thanked us for calling an election; not one person thanked us for going through with the Budget. Nobody." Gogarty betrayed the Greens' misunderstanding of the mood of the electorate at this point: "We thought if we announce we're leaving, we'll make people happy that there's going to be an election," he said. Gogarty said if the party had pulled out of Government that November it would have caused instability, and was stunned when the Greens themselves were accused of creating that instability.

Sargent revealed that the TDs and Senators had had to move quickly because they were in danger of being overtaken by events outside their control. The party leadership was once again in a bind because of the Greens' democratic tradition. According to Sargent, chaos would have ensued if they had not have made the announcement on 22 November. "At the time of the EU-IMF discussions there was considerable anger around the country in the ranks of the Green Party membership. And had we not on 22 November called time and effectively set the termination of the Government in train, there's every likelihood that the following weekend the RDS would have been booked, a large members conference would have been there and we would have seen chaos," he said. Rank and file members were frankly telling the party leadership that they no longer had their sanction to remain on in Government, so the leadership effectively cut the membership off at the pass with its announcement and commitment to passing the Budget and four-year-plan. "The decision that we took was a decision to take account of what was practical and possible, as well as what was necessary," Sargent said.

Sargent said he was convinced that pulling out of Government on 22 November would have been as dangerous as not proceeding with the bank guarantee scheme. "The considered view in the Green Party was: that's it. This is too serious. There needs to be an election," he said. "But to pull [out of Government] on 22

November would have created the kind of catastrophic knock-on effect that would be similar, in my estimation, to not having the bank guarantee," he said. The idea of calling an immediate election and not engaging with the IMF, not implementing a Budget and long-fingering the four-year plan at a time when uncertainty was rife seemed just plain wrong, he added. "The message that would have sent out to companies like Intel, never mind to the European Central Bank and to the financial markets, would have been: this country is completely irresponsible."

Ryan insisted the Greens were trying to act in the national interest, but conceded most people simply did not approve of or at least did not feel comfortable with the way the party acted that day. "They did not like the way in which the announcement was made, the sense of instability that day, that Monday," Ryan said. He described the move as "political suicide" from a Green point of view, "because we're looking to bring down the Government in a way that people don't quite like; we're at the same time putting through a Budget that people will hate." The party could not see any other remotely feasible option however, he said. "What do you do? What's the other call?" Geoghegan said the Greens knew and accepted the Government had to come to an end soon. "But at the same time we don't want to mess things up. We really don't want to mess up what could be a very difficult period in Irish life, so we decided to stay in for a Budget and all that," he said. The party was fully aware of what the electoral consequences of their actions would be, Geoghegan said. "We knew that would be an added nail in our coffin … we knew we were going to do ourselves damage," he added. However, he said one benefit was an immediate reduction in the threat of civil unrest. "By standing up there and saying, we're doing the honourable thing; we're doing the right thing, we knew at the time we wouldn't be thanked for that, but it was actually sincere that we did fear civil unrest. We didn't burst that bubble but we took some of the heat out of the situation by saying, look, this show is over after Christmas: people will have a chance to have their say."

Gogarty also contended that the Greens were motivated by a desire to pour oil on troubled waters. "We wanted to diffuse this civil unrest that we thought might happen, and violence … we felt that in announcing we were leaving, it would deflate the bubble a little bit," he said. Ryan believed the Greens succeeded in removing an increasing level of toxicity from Leinster House. "I think ultimately what it did as well is [let off] the political steam in the Dáil. That Dáil as a venue was becoming really toxic. You even had a sense of people at the gates of the Dáil. One of the things that we did was just dilute right that down. Everyone said, OK there's going to be an election early in the New Year." Not everyone was quite so sanguine about the situation, obviously.

Gormley and Ryan took a verbal pasting from Lenihan and other Fianna Fáil Ministers at the following day's Cabinet meeting. "That Cabinet meeting the next day was not an easy one," Ryan admitted. "It was difficult with Fianna Fáil; they were not happy," he said. These tensions remained constant for the next few months although some semblance of a working relationship was eventually restored, although "not a great one, an easy one." Ryan worried that his special relationship with Lenihan was over, and communications between the pair did dwindle, but he comforted himself with the belief that the experienced Minister for Finance must have had some sense of the political difficulty the Greens were in at that time in terms of pressure from their grassroots. Lenihan's distinctive voice had often boomed out of the speaker phone device in the middle of the table at Green parliamentary party meetings, during which he was happy to take any number of questions from the party's TDs and Senators and respond at some length, but that practice was discontinued.

The draconian Budget passed in early December, but the Finance Bill needed to be enacted in order to implement its terms. What the Green strategy did achieve was that it bought some time for the Government and carried the shaky administration into the New Year, but that did nothing to aid its unpopularity and the Coalition quickly faced accusations that it was stalling on holding the promised election. The Greens made things worse by attempting a final push for some of their longed-for legislation, namely the Climate Change Bill; the Mayoral Bill; the Corporate Donations Bill and Environment Bill dealing with waste levies. It was once again a terrible underestimation of the impatience of the electorate. Ryan said: "When it came to January ... I think there then was a sense that we were going to extend it out forever and a day. That was not our intention at all ... and to a certain extent while we had said put the Budget through, you also put through the Mayoral Bill the Climate Bill and so on because, Jesus, the Bills are done: get them out." Even the Greens' own supporters began to suspect them of clinging on to power for its own sake, Boyle said. "They were buying the mythology that we were hanging on.

We had already decided that we were leaving Government," he protested.

Tense discussions over an election date continued between the Greens and Fianna Fáil. Ryan said: "There was a lot of wrangling between ourselves and Fianna Fáil as to when it would be. We were insisting, I was insisting, the election has to be before the end of March." In contrast, some Fianna Fáil deputies were advocating a policy of holding off on an election, saying they preferred canvassing "with the sun on our backs," when they naively believed they would get a better reception on the doorsteps. Ryan was getting increasingly exasperated at their attitude: "Doesn't matter that it's dark; doesn't matter that it's cold. Public confidence won't stretch any further than that. That sense that the sun will rise on 1 April and we'll all be in a different mood?" He was adamant that the election had to take place well before the EU-ECB-IMF troika was due to complete its first formal review of the bailout package in mid-April. "And that's what happened. We agree there's going to be an election in March. Definite. No more nonsense," Ryan said.

Meanwhile however, Cowen was facing increasing internal pressure from TDs and Senators who continued to feel uncomfortable in the aftermath of 'Golfgate' and believed a change of leadership could restore their party's credibility with the electorate and, crucially, help them retain their seats. Cowen challenged his detractors to speak to him directly, rather than whispering in corners as many had been doing, and he sounded out the members of his large political party by telephone, disturbing Longford Westmeath TD Mary O'Rourke in the middle of a hairdressing appointment. Significantly, Micheál Martin was clearly not on board. Cowen's supporters attempted to rally the Taoiseach's flagging spirits, telling him if he stepped down he risked being remembered as "the disgraced former taoiseach who floundered over a game of golf with Anglo." On 18 January, in what seemed at the time like an inspired if unprecedented idea, he initiated a self-imposed motion of confidence in his own leadership of Fianna Fáil. Martin said he would be voting against the motion and that it was time for a change of leadership.

The Greens could do nothing but step back and let their Coalition partners attempt to sort out the internal strife that had been convulsing the party for months, although they believed the timing was preposterous. "I mean, it's mad when you think about the whole thing," Ryan said, "a leadership challenge in Fianna Fáil." Sargent recalled a sense of treading water. "It was a wait and see game really. There was no game plan or no plan B up our sleeves. Again we were focused on getting the Finance Bill [through] and could these guys please get their act together and stop distracting all of us from the work in hand," he said. "So we just stood back so that we wouldn't add to the problems. We couldn't solve their own problems for them but we could do as much as possible not to add to them." Cowen was victorious in the motion of confidence with a secret ballot, following a strong defence of his personal reputation, and Martin resigned from his Cabinet as a consequence. Cowen himself took over Martin's responsibilities at the Department of Foreign Affairs.

In the background, the Greens had been pushing their legislation again, particularly the Climate Change Bill, which they still hoped to see enacted along with the Finance Bill. It was the most important of their sponsored Bills in terms of the legacy it would leave behind for the party, and the Greens now realised their remaining time in office could be very short indeed. Ciaran Cuffe had been tasked with steering the proposed legislation through the Oireachtas. Although the proposals had been watered down, still the Green Party had faced opposition from powerful lobby groups including the Irish Business and Employers' Confederation (Ibec) and the Irish Farmers Association (IFA), with the IFA deriding the Greens as "irrational."

Ryan described the negotiations around the Bill as the most difficult the Greens had ever been involved in. "A real tricky one, the Climate Bill … really tough, down-to-the-wire stuff," he recalled. "We were facing opposition not just from the Department of Finance but from the IFA and Ibec. It's not easy stuff when you've got the whole kit and kaboodle arguing against you." Needless to say, Fianna Fáil Oireachtas members were among those who also opposed the measures, arguing that emission reduction targets would damage the agriculture sector. "And for what in reality as a Bill was sensible in my mind, the kind of scare stuff and lack of understanding of these complex issues is sometimes very difficult,"

Ryan said. Finally, however, approval came from the top ranks of the Fianna Fáil party. The Cabinet rubber-stamp made Ryan sigh with relief. "We had just got it agreed. We'd signed off on the legislation and that was a great sense of achievement. That was one of those hard won, really difficult ones and I remember a sense of, 'thank God' because that was for us, for me, a critical piece of legislation," Ryan recalled.

Dissatisfaction in the lower ranks of Fianna Fáil rumbled on, however, something which Boyle believed the leadership did nothing to prevent, as had been the case with the stag hunting and dog breeding legislation, in his view. The Greens managed to secure a high-level meeting with their Coalition partners to discuss differences with the proposed legislation and attempt to iron out any remaining difficulties. Cowen, his Minister for Defence Tony Killen and John Curran, who had replaced Pat Carey as Government whip, were due to meet Gormley, Ryan and Sargent on Wednesday morning, 19 January. The outcome of the Fianna Fáil leadership vote was also on the agenda, as was a timetable for other outstanding legislation. The Greens were feeling increasingly impotent about their inability to persuade Cowen to name a date for the General Election, so they intended to push on that as well. As frequently happens in political meetings, the 'any other business' slot at the conclusion of the one-and-a-half hour meeting would be the one to watch out for, however. Cowen had something particularly important to put to his Coalition partners.

In preparation for this important appointment, the Greens held a parliamentary party meeting on Tuesday afternoon in Ryan's office. Sargent had experienced the onset of flu-like symptoms while canvassing in Malahide. A shivering Sargent, who turned up at Ryan's office wearing a woolly hat and scarf, told his colleagues he did not feel well enough to chair their meeting or attend the meeting with the Taoiseach and his colleagues the next morning. He asked Boyle to take his place and the Corkman readily agreed. Sargent went home and, by now flattened with a full-on flu, slept for a record 12 hours straight. He often got by on six hours. The political world would look very different when he woke up.

Chapter 14

Governing in a parallel universe

"Brian Cowen is back: bigger and better than ever," Eamon Ryan recalled. Dan Boyle said the Greens were pleased that the fog of despair that enveloped the Taoiseach had appeared to lift in the immediate aftermath of his victory in the self-imposed motion of confidence in his leadership of Fianna Fáil. "We were happy to see him being more confident and assertive," he said.

The meeting between the high-level Fianna Fáil and Green Party delegations about difficulties between the Coalition partners on the Green-sponsored Climate Change Bill took place as arranged on Wednesday, 19 January 2011. Ryan, Boyle and John Gormley lined up against Cowen, Tony Killeen and John Curran. "There were a number of issues on the agenda … I think somebody mentioned the possibility of a reshuffle and that came up as the last item we were talking about," Ryan said. Cowen's rather bizarre idea was that Ministers who were not contesting the apparently rapidly approaching General Election would resign immediately and be replaced by Fianna Fáil representatives promoted from the junior Ministerial or possibly even backbench ranks.

Ryan set out what he saw as the flaws associated with the

idea of reshuffling Cabinet Ministers at this late stage of the Government's life. "It would just dint public confidence further, everyone tripping off to the Park. How could you possibly argue that new Ministers would be able to have any control of their brief in the timelines that we were talking about? It did not make sense," he said. Boyle said when the reshuffle concept was floated the Greens left their Coalition partners in no doubt about their opinion of the idea. It would look like an attempt to prolong the life of the Government, and create the impression that jobs were being distributed for political advantage. "I'm quite emphatic about what I said. I said a Cabinet change of this nature would be seen as a vote of confidence in the Government and we can't support that. We had already decided in November that the Government was coming to an end anyway so it was just a question of timing, and the idea of people resigning and having their positions filled was something we found appalling," said Boyle. Gormley already knew about Cowen's madcap plan, and had made his views known to the Taoiseach, so he left it to Ryan to do most of the talking. "We could not have been clearer. We said it in the most unequivocal fashion. Eamon Ryan was very forceful in his delivery, and he said this was not a good idea; this sent out all of the wrong signals," Gormley said. "I can tell you, we had expected that we would be listened to."

The Greens departed the meeting believing they had knocked the notion on its head, although speculation that Cowen would mount an extensive reshuffle of his Cabinet in the face of all logic continued to swirl around the nooks and crannies of Leinster House. Trevor Sargent was still down with the flu, but from what he gathered in conversations with his Green colleagues the reshuffle threat had been averted at the meeting.

"It hadn't gone brilliantly, but it had at least established that we weren't going to stand idly by and allow positions to be filled in that fashion," Sargent said. And yet, as Ryan said, the two delegations appeared to have come away with such different understandings of what had or had not been agreed about a reshuffle.

"We obviously left that meeting thinking that that's not going to happen. They, for whatever reason, and again you learn lessons in terms of clarity of decision making, left thinking that we can proceed with that," Ryan said. "Then it went absolutely mad."

In reality, the emboldened Taoiseach understood fully that the Greens had disapproved of his plan, and how it would be perceived, but he simply did not care. There was a long-standing convention in Coalition Governments that leaders of respective parties within the administration could chose their own personnel, and he was determined to stick to that no matter what. He was giving the Greens a taste of the medicine they had forcefully administered to him on 22 November, when they suddenly told him they were leaving Government just minutes before they informed the media. And what better way to do it than to schedule the announcements to take place when the enemy, as the Greens had now become, was asleep? Cowen believed he had the Greens over a barrel with their desire to implement at least the Climate Change Bill. They would not bail out now. He paid no heed to Paul Gogarty's claim that day the Green Party was prepared to sacrifice its own legislative aims to facilitate an earlier election.

News of Mary Harney's resignation broke at around 8.45 pm that same night. It had been an open secret that the Independent Minister of Health would not contest the election, so the Greens did not get too twitchy, although speculation about a wider reshuffle continued to circulate. In fact, Boyle tried to look for the positive in the announcement. "We didn't react when Mary Harney resigned because she was an Independent member and on it's own it was a positive signal, we thought, in terms of the ability of the Government at least to signal a few different things in terms of health policy," Boyle said. Gormley's wife, Penny, told him she had seen the announcement about Harney on the nine o'clock news. He was non-plussed, given that he had spoken to Harney on the Ministerial corridor that day but she had not uttered a word about her intentions or given as much as a hint that any dramatic news was coming: "No indication whatsoever," he stressed. The late evening news was also Ryan's source of the information. Sargent said he was not surprised, at the time or subsequently, that Harney had not hinted at her move. She had form, given her shock resignation from the leadership of the PDs in September 2006, and she now had no trusted colleagues she could risk confiding in at Cabinet.

When Gormley had appeared on the early evening news on that day, he appeared to sanction a mini-reshuffle but only to fill vacancies such as the one left by Micheal Martin, who had resigned from Cabinet after Cowen won the Fianna Fáil leadership vote. He also mentioned Dermot Ahern's state of health. Ahern had developed a type of rheumatoid arthritis which meant he had great difficulty walking distances and was on heavy medication. This had copper-fastened his decision to leave politics at the next election, something which he had announced on the last day of November 2010. Nevertheless, an outraged Ahern phoned Gormley after the 6 pm news and gave him a dressing down. "Dermot Ahern did take exception to that. [He] rung me, said he was quite capable of performing his duties," Gormley said. The Green leader was somewhat taken aback by the forcefulness of Ahern's intervention and told his colleagues about just how angry the Fianna Fáil Minister had been. "He was furious," Boyle said. Ahern had spoken to Gormley "in a fairly bullish way, as he can," Sargent said.

The Greens decided that, given the strength of Ahern's conviction, they might be getting a little paranoid. "I took it from that that there was going to be a continuation," Gormley recalled. Everyone knew they were in the dying days of the administration, after all, and it had seemed like such a wacky proposal. So they decided the danger of a wider reshuffle must have receded. But the plan had not been spiked, and the resignations of Ahern, Noel Dempsey and Killeen followed "in fairly rapid order" later that night. Mary White went into a radio studio shortly before 10 pm knowing only that Harney was gone and emerged an hour later to hear three more Ministers had followed the former PD leader out the Cabinet door. The announcement had been made just minutes before 11 pm. Cowen had perhaps given Harney a head-start to allow her to get coverage on the nine o'clock news, and to throw the Greens off the scent. Now the members of the junior Coalition partner, or at least those of them who were still awake, were furious. "The other three we knew were totally contrived," Boyle said. "They were all asked to leave. I'm convinced of it."

The resignations had been choreographed, leaving the Greens feeling utterly disrespected by their Coalition partners. "That's what really upset us: that there was a co-ordination about achieving all these vacancies and to fill them up," Boyle said.

Sargent was not given to sarcasm, but even he said: "It was a remarkable appearance of choreography that all these guys would troop out and say, 'We're resigning by the way, coincidentally, like our friends.'" The Greens, and other onlookers, could not believe what was happening. "It just seemed like there was a parallel universe going on in Government," Sargent said. The Greens felt particularly betrayed by Dempsey: they had believed he was their friend, or at least the closest thing Fianna Fáil had to a closeted Green, and thought he might at least have tipped them off. The Greens said Killeen had sat through a meeting with them that morning and said nothing, although the Fianna Fáil man later said he learned he would be resigning at that meeting and went back to his office and wrote a formal resignation letter.

Gormley had taken one of his famous early nights and had

not heard the news about Ahern, Dempsey and Killeen until he turned on the radio at 7 am on Thursday morning. He promptly rang Cowen, expressing what he described as "surprise and dismay." Boyle said he was told the conversation was "testy." The Green parliamentary party assembled at 9.30 am, then Gormley, Ryan and White met the Taoiseach twice. The tone of the meeting was formally courteous but extremely tense. Fianna Fáil was not for turning. "They swear blind that we didn't say what we were saying. They didn't want to hear," Boyle said. "I think it was because it wasn't put in the context of 'No No No.'" But Ryan, with his mild-mannered presentation style, was no Ian Paisley, despite Gormley's assertion that Ryan had delivered "one of the most forceful speeches I remember Eamon ever giving."

The Greens were not alone in their assessment of the bizarre situation. Many Fianna Fáil parliamentarians, including Ministers, were as repulsed by Cowen's idea as members of the junior Coalition party had been. "He's after destroying the party tonight," one prominent young Fianna Fáil TD said. Minister of State for Children Barry Andrews, who was phoned at home after midnight and offered the justice portfolio, he had the sense to decline. Rebuffing the offer, he explained that he did not want to be seen to be abandoning his own portfolio so late in the day. Ryan believed Cowen must have wanted to make some kind of "grand gesture" before the election, but this was misjudged move was undoubtedly a blunder. Boyle said: "The thinking was Brian Cowen wanted to reinvent his Fianna Fáil team going into an election with fresh faces, but given what he had done in his original Cabinet appointment that was no cause for confidence. The people he had appointed in the first instance did not inspire us."

Boyle and the other Greens had certainly welcomed Cowen's change of attitude following his victory in the Fianna Fáil leadership vote, and the buoyed-up Taoiseach put in a welcome return-to-form performance during Wednesday morning's Leaders Questions. "But he let it go to his head though, that's the thing," Boyle said. "I suppose you could put it down to the fact that he had such a feeling of elation and relief at having won a Fianna Fáil vote of confidence, a parliamentary party vote of confidence, that he seemed to assume that that was a Government vote of confidence and the Government was Fianna Fáil," he said. "He just went bull-headed from then on in." Boyle said Cowen had calculated the Greens would remain on in Government until they got the Climate Change Bill passed, "and they could do whatever they wanted: that was a classic misassumption." Sargent said the Greens had not wanted to turn the disagreement over the reshuffle plan into a "public ordeal," but trust had broken down so completely. "When your coalition partner says it would be a mistake, it doesn't sound like any form of agreement going on there. When they said it would go down like a lead balloon, that's pretty clear. And then having to say, if it goes to the Dáil we won't vote for it, that's kind of confrontational never mind disagreement, and we were trying to avoid confrontation," he said.

News of Batt O'Keeffe's resignation filtered through on

Thursday, after denials. He was a close friend of the Taoiseach. Cowen finally accepted the Greens were serious when they said they could not vote in favour of a reshuffle in the Dáil, which meant he would be unable to make the new appointments to Cabinet, and he cursed the Greens for vetoing the appointments. They had changed the arrangements that had always applied to Coalition Governments, he thundered, and had overridden his Constitutional prerogative as Taoiseach. RTÉ news presenter Bryan Dobson would put it up to the Taoiseach that evening: "Your authority is on its knees," he suggested. Cowen clearly continued to see nothing wrong with his aborted plan however, claiming he believed it would in fact be cynical to leave retiring ministers in office. In the Dáil on Thursday afternoon, Cowen set the general election date for Friday, 11 March and reassigned the now vacant portfolios to existing ministers, many of whom ended up double-jobbing because the number of Cabinet Ministers was so low. There were nine Ministers instead of the usual 15, and who would have thought two of those last standing would be Green. Throughout their time in office, the Greens had been accused of propping up the Fianna Fáil-led administration. Their protestations that this was not the case were becoming more and more difficult to believe.

Cowen reassigned the Department of Health and Children to his Tánaiste Mary Coughlan and gave Ahern's justice portfolio to the Minister for Agriculture Brendan Smith. Dempsey's transport portfolio was assigned to the Minister for Community and Family Affairs Pat Carey, while Killeen's defence portfolio went to the Minister for Social Protection Eamon Ó Cuív. The Minister for Tourism Mary Hanafin took over the enterprise, trade and innovation brief, which was O'Keeffe's old job. Jokes about moving the deck chairs on the Titanic abounded. Backers of Martin huddled together in clusters around Leinster House, apparently no longer caring that they could be seen and heard by journalists.

The Greens knew they had to kiss goodbye to hopes of ever seeing enacted their most cherished proposals, even the ones relating to climate change. Publicly they continued to insist that some of the legislation they had sponsored would be passed, but the Greens knew only the Finance Bill, to enact the terms of the Government, now would be prioritised given the level bitterness between the Coalition partners. Sargent likened the state of the relationship between the Greens and Fianna Fáil to that of a couple with children going through a painful separation process. "It was pretty much breaking down and it came down to the Finance Bill. It was like a couple separating and saying, 'What about the children? Let's stay together to get the children sorted,' and the child was the Finance Bill," he said. "Climate change and corporate donations and the Mayoral Bill: they were like children that we were planning to adopt but we decided not to go ahead because they wouldn't have had a good upbringing against that background," he joked. "Hopefully they'll find a good home when the next marriage made in heaven happens."

Shortly after 4 pm on Thursday, a text was sent to political correspondents. "The Green Party will present an explanation of today's events at a press conference in the Merrion Hotel at 4.45 pm," it said. In the luxury hotel where the IMF delegation had lodged in November, across the road from Leinster House, the Greens announced they were staying in Government. Gormley insisted the country needed the stability the Finance Bill would provide. "The politically opportune thing for the Green Party to do would be to skedaddle," he said. Meanwhile, tears were trickling down Sargent's face. Panicking that the cameras would pick up on the fact, Sargent swiped his hand across his cheek, giving his face a sheen that the strong lights bounced off. "And then the tweeting started … was Trevor Sargent crying at that press conference?" He denied it strenuously and blamed "the lingering symptoms of man flu."

On Saturday, a shattered-looking Cowen would stand where the Greens had sat in the Merrion Hotel just two days earlier. Looking pale and pitiful, he announced he had decided "on my own counsel" to resign as Fianna Fáil leader but remain on as Taoiseach, a situation he had previously regarded as ridiculous and no doubt still did. It was difficult for the Greens to watch a man so humbled, but the announcement was not a complete shock to them, because at around 11 am that morning a "slightly coded" message had been passed from Fianna Fáil to the Greens, indicating that Cowen was finally going, Sargent said. The Dublin North TD and his team interrupted a canvassing session in

Balbriggan to watch events unfold on television in a local hotel, where "they reluctantly switched over from Sky Sports." Warming mugs of tea and coffee were ordered. "And so we settled ourselves down … to witness history in the making," he recalled. The series of momentous events had left Sargent with an unsettling feeling akin to traveling in a vehicle that was out of control. "Just another wheel falling off the car, really, and we're still rolling along," he said. "So that was another breakdown, I guess, another reason to feel the confidence ebbing away."

Ryan too was watching the latest developments live on television. He also felt worn down after the last number of years during which the country had lurched from one economic crisis to another. The Greens had repeatedly insisted they were only staying on in Government in order to get the Finance Bill through, and now it looked as if not even that was going to happen. "That day my sense was … now it's a political mess and we don't even have the Budget through," Ryan said. "That to a certain extent we saw as the way of getting the country out of the crisis," he added. Ryan reached out once again to an old ally, placing a call to Simon Coveney of Fine Gael. The bond they had forged during their many walks together around Merrion Square, where they had gone when they needed to escape the toxic atmosphere of Leinster House, remained strong. "I rang Simon Coveney at about one o'clock and said to him, 'Is there a way in which we can still get the Finance Bill through so that the Budget is completed?'" Ryan had called senior officials in the Department of Finance on Thursday and Friday, "and said, 'Is it a problem if it doesn't get through?' And it really clearly was."

After speaking to Coveney, his next phone call was to Brian Lenihan. He got a cooler reception from the Fianna Fáil man, but Lenihan said he would make a call. "And then in fairness to both of them – Simon Coveney rang Enda [Kenny] and Brian Lenihan talked to Brian Cowen – and they pretty much agreed by six that evening that we would agree a process by which we would get the Finance Bill through," he said.

Fine Gael's finance spokesman "kind of hinted" that progress could be made and a proposed motion of confidence in the Government dropped when he appeared on the television news.

The Greens had a plan to meet in Gormley's house the day after Cowen resigned, but decided at the last minute to divert to Government Buildings for 11.30 am. They were anxious not to alert the media to their presence. "We'd half expected there might be a posse of journalists and cameramen outside, so there were watches being kept and I was getting calls and texts saying, 'You can come in the normal way. All seems quiet on the Western front,'" Sargent said. The reason for the lack of media personnel was because the early morning radio news had said the party was already meeting, although no-one was quite sure where. When Sargent heard this he was impressed at what the party's communications team had cooked up. He thought they had been clever to indicate the meeting was already underway, so reporters would give up, temporarily, on trying to hunt down the Greens.

Sargent normally travelled to the city centre by train, often with his fold-up bicycle, but on this exceptional morning he adopted a mode of transport the Greens usually frowned on and drove his car to Government Buildings, parking in one of the spaces normally reserved for Ministerial Mercedes. There were plenty of free spaces, as it was a Sunday. The TDs and Senators squeezed into Donall Geoghegan's long and narrow office, with its asylum-white walls, where they were joined by party staffers and the communications team. A big decision had to be taken and the process of arriving at that decision proved difficult because opinion was divided even at this very late stage. The atmosphere at the meeting was "very intense … it was heavy," Boyle recalled. "There were raised voices; there was loose language; there was tension that might have resulted in emotional release." It was inevitable someone would crack. The newest member of the group, Mark Dearey, a Senator for just 11 months, found the discussions particularly hard going, and the soft-centred Dundalk man broke down in tears. The Greens were in an "awful dilemma," White said.

"The debate we had was exhausting." The word from the National Executive Council, which was directly elected by party members and which had met that morning, was that rank and file members were in open revolt at the administration's continuation. The grassroots were inundating the Green parliamentarians with texts and emails telling them in no uncertain terms that the time to leave Government was long past.

Sargent's mind was clear. "The mood was very frank ... Each of us was asked to really think this through. Could we continue on? Was this the right time to go?" Everyone knew Gormley's position: he had wanted to the Greens to leave Government for a long time at this stage but his colleagues had argued forcefully against him. Sargent, as a former leader, had remained out of the argument, but at that meeting he broke with that convention. Having made it very clear that they no longer had confidence in the Government, it was not tenable for the Greens to continue as part of the administration, he argued. "No point asking hypothetical questions like should we have done something earlier, but was this the time? And I was certainly convinced that this was the time, and the majority were," Sargent said. Two prominent members of the Green's parliamentary group wanted the party to remain in power, however.

Ryan and Ciaran Cuffe were in the minority. The pair – two of the four who would have to write letters of Ministerial resignation if the Greens pulled out – wanted to stay in Government for legacy and policy reasons. "Ciaran and Eamon, who are very policy focused, and delivering in Government and the consequences are secondary; it's the legacy of what we can do given this opportunity, which is valid and we all explored that. And then we explored the other," Sargent said. "So in the end we unanimously agreed."

But was the decision really unanimous? "Well it was, because a consensus is what was arrived at and the nature of the consensus is that it develops in the course of the discussions," Sargent claimed. Boyle said a weight appeared to lift from Gormley's shoulders. "It was a release for John once the decision was made," Boyle recalled. "I don't think any of us will ever experience anything like that in our life again."

The Wesley Suite in the Merrion Hotel was booked for 3.30 pm, and a text message was sent to political correspondents 45 minutes in advance. A few formalities, such as Ministerial resignations, had to be taken care of first, however. The shell-shocked Greens got up from the mahogany table where the momentous decision had finally been made and wandered around individually or in pairs. "I remember us preparing to go over to the Merrion Hotel. We had made a decision, we knew what was happening. We had to wait for John and Eamon and Ciaran and Mary to get their resignation letters together, and we were just walking up and down the corridor," Boyle said. "We were letting things sink in and I suppose we were a bit shell shocked as well, like. It was a weird atmosphere," he said. Informing the Taoiseach and Fianna Fáil Ministers also took a little time, because of what Gormley described as the "fragmentation" in the party. Although there were not very many Fianna Fáil Ministers left, three of them – Mary Hanafin, Brian Lenihan and Éamon Ó Cuív – were by now in competition for the position of party leader, along with Micheál Martin.

Meanwhile, the Greens had kept the jittery media waiting, and kept them guessing. A hush came over the chattering pack when Gormley finally poked his head around the door of the Wesley Suite. Reporters were shocked at his poor colouring: he looked waxy and completely drained of energy. He approached the podium which had replaced the long table the party had used three days previously, and his colleagues clustered around him supportively. The microphones went live. "Are you ready?" Boyle asked Gormley. "Yeah," Gormley replied.

"For a very long time we in the Green Party have stood back in the hope that Fianna Fáil could resolve persistent doubts about their party leadership. A definitive resolution of this has not yet been possible and our patience has reached an end. Because of these continuing doubts, the lack of communication and the breakdown in trust, we have decided that we can no longer continue in Government," he said. He announced that the Greens would now support a "truncated" Finance Bill from the Opposition benches and appealed for "some level of bipartisanship in order to get an early election." When Gormley finished answering questions, Mary White whispered an encouraging: "Well done John." Niall Ó Brolcháin went further: "Brilliant," he said.

And yet the uncertainty continued, because while the Greens' announcement meant that the General Election would take place earlier than 11 March, the new date of the election was not yet confirmed, although February 25 was speculated about if a timetable to pass the Finance Bill could be agreed. There were now just seven people in Cabinet, the absolute minimum allowed under the Constitution. Cowen assigned the responsibilities of Gormley and Ryan to two of the Ministers who remained in place. Carey took on Ryan's Communications, Energy and Natural Resources brief, which he juggled along with the Transport portfolio and his position as Minister for Community and Family Affairs. Ó Cuív was assigned Gormley's Environment portfolio, which added to his workload as Minister for Defence who also had responsibility for the Department of Social Protection. The situation had gone beyond farcical.

Lenihan formally invited the Greens and the Opposition parties to enter his Department of Finance offices on Monday afternoon to discuss how the Finance Bill might be passed, Ryan recalled. Sinn Fein's finance spokesman Pearse Doherty left the meeting saying a "grubby little deal" had been hatched inside, but Fine Gael's Michael Noonan and Labour's Joan Burton seemed somewhat more content. "I was really proud of that because at least in the very chaotic year, where politics hadn't exactly worked and you hadn't got national consensus, effectively you got national consensus at that meeting in that, OK Sinn Fein played it, kind of stormed out, but Labour and Fine Gael effectively agreed," Ryan said. The path had been cleared for a General Election on February 25. "And that, at least from my perspective, in what had been a terrible year of political failings, when the public had lost confidence in the political system, was at least the political system showing that it was able to have a transfer of power while at the same time managing the budgetary process that did need to be managed, and in an sense taking collective responsibility."

Ryan comforted himself with the belief that some sort of outcome had been achieved. The appearance of the Green parliamentarians changed almost instantly, and they relaxed back into the more casual clothes and slightly crumpled appearance they had sported before they entered Government.

IT WAS AGREED THAT THE SEANAD WOULD MEET ON THE FOLLOWING Friday and Saturday to approve the legislation. During Friday's debate, Lenihan said he found it extraordinary that the Green Party "couldn't find it in their hearts" to stay in Government for an extra week to allow time for tax changes affecting civil partners to be included in the Bill. Boyle and Lenihan had what the former described as a "huge run in" that day. "He did work well with John and Eamon ... but after we'd left Government his attitude changed significantly. We had this set-to in the Seanad anteroom on the Finance Bill ... he just turned on me and what he actually said was, 'It's because of your party that the country's in the state it's in,'" Boyle said. "That was practically the last thing he said to me," he added, sadly. "It was a flavour of the time."

CHAPTER 15

WATERLOO OR DUNKIRK?

ON 3 FEBRUARY, THE GREEN PARTY'S FORMER MINISTERS, TDs and Senators gathered in a nightclub off St Stephen's Green in Dublin. It was 10 o'clock in the morning.

Someone in the party's back room team had chosen the Sugar Club, a former cinema, as the location for their campaign launch for the 2011 General Election. Reporters stumbled in, blinking until their eyes adjusted to the darkness, and were directed towards the red velvet couches. The bar was closed, but a selection of fruit was on offer.

John Gormley spoke from a podium on the stage, with the party's election slogan, 'Renewing Ireland', projected in pink letters on a green screen behind him, while Eamon Ryan and Trevor Sargent shared a little cocktail table to his right, and Dan Boyle and Mark Dearey perched in a similar fashion on his left.

Opinion polls were by now predicting a Fine Gael-Labour Government was practically the only possible result of the election, but Gormley insisted the outcome remained far from certain. He warned voters against granting the coalition a "bloated majority." Surprisingly, he even went as far as to suggest that the Greens could serve alongside Fine Gael and Labour in a new coalition administration. Reporters had to double-check this was what he had actually intended to say.

"We feel that, yes, we can make a contribution and a very important contribution to a future Government. We've always said that we would be happy to serve in a rainbow coalition and that remains our ambition. We wanted to do it the last time; it wasn't possible. But we would bring to that Government imagination, experience and a proven track record of creating jobs," he said. Gormley predicted "a clash of egos as well as a clash of policies" between Fine Gael leader Enda Kenny and Labour Party leader Eamon Gilmore if they went into government together. "If the Greens got in there maybe we could keep them apart a little bit and get a bit of sanity," he said.

Indicating that the Greens had perhaps retained some of their once famous naivete, Gormley fell hook, line and sinker for a cheeky question from the *Daily Mail*'s political editor Senan Moloney, who speculated that the party might be "incinerated" in the approaching election. Gormley obligingly insisted he was "not contemplating any incineration" of his party, giving the chuckling reporter exactly the quote he wanted.

Gormley acknowledged it would be a "very tough" election for Green Party candidates, but boldly predicted the six TDs would be returned and insisted he believed that gains could be made. The nine members of the parliamentary party would be fighting for the last seat, often with Fianna Fáil, in their constituencies, he said, but this would be nothing new for the Greens, who always had "to dig our seats out of granite" in every election.

Despite his overtures to Fine Gael and Labour, Gormley vigorously attacked their pre-election proposals. He criticized Fine Gael's plan for voluntary public sector redundancies in addition to those previously outlined by the Government. He said 30,000 jobs could not be cut in three years with only limited cuts to services. Labour had abandoned its key taxation policy of a third rate of 48 per cent and was "dodging and fudging crunch issues," Gormley claimed. While the Greens had experienced difficulties with Fianna Fáil when they were in coalition, Fine Gael and Labour did not understand "the mechanics of government". Gormley also said the Greens were the only party that could be trusted on climate change, sustainability and the creation of "real green jobs." He said the Greens' vision extended beyond the horizon of the next general election."

Gormley also managed, for perhaps the first time, to articulate quite concisely his party's achievements in Government, in response to a question from *Sunday Times'* political editor Stephen O'Brien who asked if the Greens were not hamstrung by leaving Government without fulfilling key legislative aims. "Our record of delivery stands up to scrutiny … the whole question of the planning legislation, which was I think ground-breaking; what Eamon has done in relation to renewables … civil partnership;

protecting education. These are very important issues," Gormley said. He could also have mentioned Ryan's work on the broadband sector.

Ryan, meanwhile, said Fine Gael's policies would "destroy the ESB", adding that he "looked aghast" at that party's jobs proposals. "Back in the old days it used to be that Garret [FitzGerald] would worry that something works in practice but does it work in theory? It seems to me now that Fine Gael have loads of theory but I don't see it working in practice." Despite all this fighting talk, expectations ahead of the election were not high although many within the party remained optimistic that Sargent and, perhaps, Ryan could hold onto their seats. Donall Goeghegan said there was a realisation that the party was going to get a "pretty bad" result. Geoghegan said Gormley "would have been a little bit more realistic that some others, or maybe more pessimistic" when assessing the party's chances of seat retention. "We were going to be losing seats, the majority of our seats," he added. No-one ever really said it out loud, however, for obvious reasons.

"Obviously you don't discuss everything openly with everybody. It's an election campaign. People are going out fighting for their seats, and fighting hard, and you don't want to discourage people." However, he hoped that a pair of seats could be somehow salvaged from the impending wreckage. "You were looking at saving two at the most, that was my thinking. I thought Trevor would get across the line – I was sure Trevor would get across the line," he said. "I don't think Trevor expected to lose his seat, so it's quite upsetting to see that happening."

Geoghegan described Sargent's canvassing campaign as "second to none among not just within the Green Party but in any political party." Sargent, who Geoghegan described as the "Mr Nice Guy of the Greens," had always been able to attract transfers, but not this time. "Right towards the end there was still an off chance that he might make it, but then we saw some of the transfer numbers coming in and said no that's the end of it. So it was very disappointing." Boyle also said Sargent found electoral defeat particularly difficult. "Trevor did take that very hard," he said.

Geoghegan thought there was also a chance that Ryan would return to the Dáil. "Eamon was convinced he was going to get in. He thought he would. I thought he might," he said. "He [Ryan] worked during that campaign ... He's not a natural canvasser; he's not a natural on the doors. But he finally got it together enough to be able to go out and do his thing." Mary White was thinking along similar lines to Geoghegan. "I thought we might end up with two seats ... I thought Trevor and Eamon would be our best bet," she said. Boyle thought so too. "Even though we knew it was going to be a difficult election, we still had a hope for Eamon and Trevor," he said.

So what happened? The party fielded 43 candidates, one in every constituency in Ireland. Gormley lost his seat in Dublin South-East. He polled 2,370 first preferences, just 27 more votes than the *Independent* economist Paul Sommerville, and was eliminated on the fifth count. Gormley's constituency reflected the national mood, with voters rejecting their Government TDs: Fianna Fáil's Chris Andrews also failed to get re-elected here. Lucinda Creighton of Fine Gael topped the poll and her running mate Eoghan Murphy was also elected. Labour's Ruairi Quinn and Kevin Humphreys were the other two successful candidates in the changeable four-seat constituency.

Over in Dublin South, Ryan pulled in 4,929 first preference votes but was eliminated on the seventh count. Independent Senator Shane Ross topped the poll and was elected on the first count with a grand total of 17,075 first preferences. Labour's Alex White was also successful in Dublin South, after losing out to George Lee in the 2009 byelection. Three Fine Gael TDs were elected: Alan Shatter, Olivia Mitchell and Peter Matthews. In Dublin North, Sargent was eliminated on the fifth count after securing 4,186 votes. Successful in that constituency were Fine Gael's Dr James Reilly and Alan Farrell, Brendan Ryan of Labour and the Socialist Party candidate Clare Daly. Fianna Fáil TDs Darragh O'Brien and Michael Kennedy also lost their seats.

Paul Gogarty got just 1,484 first preferences in Dublin Mid-West and was eliminated on the sixth count in the constituency, where the successful candidates were Joanna Tuffy and Robert Dowds of Labour and Fine Gael's Frances Fitzgerald and Derek Keating. In Dun Laoghaire, Ciaran Cuffe polled 2,156 first preferences and was eliminated on the sixth count. Fianna Fáil's Mary Hanafin and Barry Andrews also lost their seats in Dun Laoghaire, where the winners were Labour's Eamon Gilmore and Fine Gael's Sean Barrett and Mary Mitchell-O'Connor, along with Richard Boyd-Barrett of the People Before Profit Alliance. In Carlow-Kilkenny, Mary White got 2,072 first preference votes and was eliminated on the seventh count. Fine Gael scored a hat trick in the constituency with Phil Hogan, John Paul Phelan and Pat Deering, while Fianna Fáil's John McGuinness held on and Labour's Ann Phelan was also elected.

In Cork South-Central, where Boyle was bidding to win back the seat he lost in 2007, he got 1,640 votes and was eliminated on the sixth count. Mark Dearey secured 3,244 votes and was eliminated on the ninth count in Louth, while Niall Ó Brolcháin got 1,120 votes in Galway West and was knocked out in the second count. So all seats were lost and no new positions secured. The party did so badly it was excluded from State funding because its support had fallen to below two per cent. Fianna Fáil, the longtime colossus of Irish politics, slumped from 72 to 20 TDs. A new Government was formed between a greatly-strengthened Fine Gael and Labour, as the polls had predicted.

Gormley soon made clear he would stand down as leader, saying so in an email to party members. It was time for a "new beginning", Gormley said, and there was a "need to get back to our roots as a radical campaigning party." Attention immediately turned to Ryan and Boyle whose names were frequently mentioned as potential successors to Gormley. Dearey's name was also floated, but he said he was concentrating on his business. Ryan was amazed when Boyle did not put his name forward, and when Gormley's successor was eventually announced on 27 May, 2011 in Party headquarters on Suffolk Street, Ryan had seen off competition from Kilkenny county councillor Malcolm Noonan and party activist Phil Kearney.

Speaking in the aftermath of his election, Ryan railed against the new Fine Gael/Labour Coalition Government's "shelving" of the Greens' climate change initiatives and specific plans to reform local government. He said his first task would be to encourage young people to join the party ahead of the 2014 local elections. He also said he wanted to "slay the myths" that the Greens were against rural development and Dublin-centric. He warned that money would be scarce for the party and said it was a time for tight belts. He said he was mostly living off the severance payments he received following his period as Minister, and hoped to get some policy work for not-for-profit organizations in the energy sector.

A relaxed-looking Gormley was there to wish Ryan well, emphasising his successor's passion, commitment and eloquence. "He's exactly the right person to lead this party into the future," Gormley said. The former leader admitted to still finding it difficult to deal with the loss of seats. "Nevertheless our spirit is undiminished," he said. On 11 June, the Greens met in the

Hilton Hotel by Dublin's Grand Canal. It was a subdued affair, talking place the day after the death of Brian Lenihan, and solemn but warm tributes were paid to him by his former colleagues in Government.

Ryan and Paul Gogarty met awkwardly at the door of the event, at which former councillor Catherine Martin, a sister of former councillor Vincent P. Martin, was elected deputy leader. Martin beat Mark Dearey and Northern Ireland Green Party activist John Barry. Gormley returned to the theme of environmentalism when he addressed the surprisingly large gathering of some 300 activists. "How can we have infinite economic growth on a finite planet? It is a total illogicality. And we're the only party. Think about this. We're the only party that asks that question," he said. "Just at the time when our message is more relevant than ever we suffered our worst electoral defeat," he added. He told party members how he had implored his parliamentary colleagues to leave Government many times, to no avail. "I want to tell this story against myself … I said to them if we go through with this Budget, making an adjustment of 6 million, that we will be absolutely finished in electoral terms. And they said we've got to do the right thing for the country," he said.

Gormley did not spare the two parties that made up the new administration. "The Opposition", as he continued to call Fine Gael and Labour, would have won the election comfortably but had conducted a "dishonest" campaign, he claimed, adding that

Lenihan had "opened the books" to them in the Department of Finance at the Green Party's request. "The election my friends was not our Waterloo; it was our Dunkirk," Gormley insisted, raising a laugh by adding: "I'm not going to compare Eamon Ryan to Churchill." Again Gormley praised Ryan's "commitment, passion and vision" and called him a "great man." Boyle would later say differences in approach between Gormley and Ryan meant relations between them were not as smooth as they might have been. "They were never too difficult but stylistically they were very different. I suppose they needed to have talked about things more and I think that might have lead occasionally to decisions being made because there wasn't a proper co-ordinated approach between the two of them at cab, but not too much," Boyle said. But it was clear that, in the aftermath of the election, any difficulties had been put aside and the mutual respect that pre-dated their time in Government remained intact.

The guest speaker at the Hilton was the Swedish MP Agneta Borjesson, who outlined how the Swedish Green Party rebuilt after enduring electoral wipeout following its first period in government. The electoral fate that befell the Irish Green Party in 2011, although traumatic for its members, was not unusual at all, it seemed. Inspired by Borjesson's contribution, Ryan predicted the Green Party would return to electoral success.

"In 20 years we should have 25 members of Dáil Éireann and follow your example," he told Borjesson. Ryan said the Greens had "friends in Europe" sharing the same philosophy, unlike other Irish political parties. He said the "road to recovery" had begun with the recent election of the cheerful Steven Agnew as an MLA to the Northern Ireland Assembly in May.

"I believe we will return to electoral success," Ryan insisted. "I've a faith in the common sense and the decency of the Irish people. I think they'll vote for us again. I think they get that the Green agenda is the best future for our country. It's our job just to unlock the potential for that to happen."

In the course of his keynote address at the conference, Ryan said the Fianna Fáil-Green administration had come to an end in an "awkward, broken way" and the junior coalition partner had suffered a "savage electoral meltdown."

"The people did not buy what we were doing and they punished us." He said the Greens had not convinced enough people of their reasons for staying in government, or of the party's strategy and message. "Whatever it took to communicate, we the parliamentary party didn't get it right and I personally take my share of the blame in that failure," he said. He called on a new generation of people to join the Greens and said there would be senior roles for women within the party, which had fielded just eight female candidates. He announced a summer gathering of environmental activists at Carnsore Point, Co. Wexford, scene of a campaign against nuclear power in the late 1970s.

Boyle stressed the Greens' connection to an international

movement, which differentiated them from most other Irish political parties. Already in April, the German Greens were once again celebrating electoral success. "It's not unique to the Irish Green Party. The Germans; the Czechs; the Swedes; the Estonians: they've all gone through a period of going into parliament and losing all parliamentary seats. It is part of the growth process, and we've never had a critical mass of votes that allowed us to be totally secure anyway," Boyle said. "We do have an international context."

Ryan recalled looking to the junior Coalition partner on Ireland's neighbouring island for succour during a particularly stressful time. At a session of the British-Irish Council on the Isle of Man in December 2010, Brian Cowen held talks with Britain's Deputy Prime Minister and leader of the Liberal Democrats Nick Clegg about the UK's contribution to Ireland's economic bailout. On the fringes of the formal session, Ryan and Clegg swapped war stories and exchanged tips for surviving in Coalition Governments.

"I was thrilled to meet him because, in a sense, there's a certain similarity of situations. And he said something very simple. He said, 'you've a real difficulty because to make Government work you've got to work with people but at the same time in a Coalition Goverment you're by nature in with a political party that your own members don't want to see you working with,'" Ryan said.

"They want you to be kicking and fighting and screaming.

And that's a dilemma that for anyone, particularly a smaller party in a Coalition Government, is a really difficult one to overcome, and it's not easy to manage and it's particularly not easy to manage at a time of economic crisis, when the party we were in with was in Government for the previous 10 years, so there's none of the get-out clause: 'It's not us; it's the previous shower.' Jesus, that's a very difficult situation."

While Ryan concentrated on the party leadership, Gormley treated himself to a much-needed holiday in his favourite location: north Wales. Sargent got behind a vegetable stall selling fresh produce at the Balbriggan farmers' market in north Dublin. Cuffe returned to lecturing, while White set up a company offering walking tours of Carlow.

Gogarty took part in a reality television show, while Boyle recorded an album of original material, including an acapella number.

Much time was spent thinking over the party's time in Government and considering what the future might hold. Cuffe had always cautioned Green colleagues against using military metaphors when talking about politics, but Gormley returned again and again to his Waterloo/Dunkirk analogy. "Inevitably, you always use military metaphors. It now means that we are outwardly at least beaten into the ground and most observers will say, that's the end of them. But I'm saying it's not necessarily the case. Waterloo was the end of Napoleon – that was it, gone – but

Dunkirk was the beginning of a fightback. That's the way I see it," he said.

"But I think we will re-emerge. I think it will be a very different party. I think the party will become far more aggressive, in a sense." A new name is not an option, he insisted, but a new attitude will prevail. "I think the party won't be taking any prisoners ever again." Gormley does not believe the fate of other now defunct small Irish political parties will befall the Greens. "We're not like the PDs. People make that comparison and it's misplaced. The PDs were a collection of individuals who had already been in politics and perhaps for their own opportunistic reasons they decided they were going to go their separate ways. That won't happen with the Green Party," he insisted.

Since the election, the Greens had continued to hear the refrain that they had propped up the Fianna Fáil-led administration. "People's main gripe with us is going into Government with Fianna Fáil and keeping Fianna Fáil in Government," Boyle said. "I would never regret going into Government. I'm happy we played a role and I think history will judge us differently; mistakes and all. We certainly weren't responsible for the policies that caused the problem ... We have to take responsibility ourselves but I'd still go into Government tomorrow." In terms of specific regrets, Boyle cited not following Gormley's advice: "What I regret is not acting on John's instinct and leaving in September [2010]. That's the time to have left," he said. Sargent too stuck to the line that the Greens had remained focused on implementing their policies. "I'd always say to people when they talk about keeping Fianna Fáil in power: it was about implementing the Programme for Government, and that was the focal point."

Looking back, both Ryan and Boyle thought they had probably spent too much time filling media slots during moments of crisis, while Fianna Fáil representatives demurred. "I think on my own part, people would have said I was out too much, but to a certain extent my sense was it was a moment of national crisis … and I felt a certain obligation … to go out and take some of those media slots," Ryan said. "As a Cabinet minister, even as an elected member of the Dáil, you cannot say, 'No sorry I don't do economics … ' but there was a real reluctance to fill those slots."

Boyle said: "Both myself and Eamon would freely admit that partly because of an unwillingness on Fianna Fáil's part, and partly a lack of ability on behalf of many of its own spokespersons, myself and Eamon found ourselves far too much in the media talking about economic policy."

If he had his time again, Boyle would be more reticent. "The media were quite happy to talk to myself and Eamon. We fell for it to a large extent, being seen as the communicators I guess … it definitely was to our detriment, it certainly was to mine anyway," he said. "It's still my inclination to be open, but I probably wouldn't be as open; I wouldn't be as forthcoming; I wouldn't be as available, and that's hard for me to say." Boyle also regretted the style of their interventions, saying they should have been much more forceful.

"I felt we should have been a lot more aggressive. That's my own inclination; that's what I was trying to do with twitter and all the rest of it. You fight your corner; you get your messages out there. We took too much stuff on the chin and too much of the mud stuck."

Boyle said the Greens had built up something like a fund of goodwill in certain sections of the media during their time in Opposition, but that evaporated in June 2007. "The day we went into Government all the goodwill we had built up over the previous decade was gone, because we became the enemy. We were in bed with Fianna Fáil and the media, for all its individual impartiality, has an anti-Fianna Fáil leaning because Fianna Fáil has been in Government for most of the time, and we suffered that backlash," he said.

Ideologues are rare in Irish politics, and it is even more unusual for a group of them to get a shot at the title in the way the Green Party did between 2007 and 2011. Observing the often painful clash between ideology and real politik throughout those years was fascinating, as is considering how many seats the Greens might have gained in 2011 if they had managed to resist the lure of power four years previously.

Within those four years, the Greens found themselves transformed in the public perception from quirky outsiders to loathed facilitators thanks to the vagaries of the proportional representation system, which can sometimes result in small parties with niche policies wielding what appears to be an inordinate amount of power. It certainly did not always feel like that to the Greens, however, as Cuffe explained. "We only had real clout within the last year year-and-a-half in Government once the PDs had disappeared off the scene, but even when you look at that clout there were six Green TDs; there was around about 80 Fianna Fáilers. You can't play your 'we're going to leave' card at every Cabinet meeting or every day of the week."

Their demolition as a parliamentary force was inevitable given the economic circumstances, and Ryan and his colleagues learned the hard way the importance of timing in politics and the dangers of ever adopting a sanctimonious tone on issues of morality.

"The kind of message, the simple message, was we were going in to get things done in a particularly green area, which is true. But I think from a public perspective [people thought] they're not actually in there for the national interest, they're in there to get things done that I don't particularly care about," he said. "In a moment of economic crisis I don't care about climate change; I don't care about good planning. Even though it is the cause of the problem in the first place it's not the immediate problem. The immediate problem is my wages are being taxed; or I'm in danger of losing my job; or my daughter may emigrate. So that general sense that the Greens were getting something for themselves but that's not what I wanted them for I just want someone to get us out of this economic crisis became somewhat reinforced." As other political parties have learned to their cost, being in Government can divert attention away from the necessary nurturing of the party.

"One of the facets of our participating in Government was that the breadth of Government swamps any small party, and there's just so much detail and we lost sight of the party because of what we saw as being our responsibility of being in Government. I think that was the biggest failure," Boyle said. He recalled feeling shocked at how little reaction in terms of emails, phone calls and letters to constituency offices the Greens received in the aftermath of the Budget in 2009.

"We'd been used to a tirade going up to that. That meant one of either two things, it meant either there was an acceptance of the situation or there was an indifference, and it was more likely the indifference had kicked in at that stage."

But in the middle of their greatest agony, at 2.52 am during RTÉ's marathon television coverage of the election count, the broadcaster and historian John Bowman had offered some kind words. "The Greens, by the way, although they've lost all their seats, the Greens have a future because they're out to save the planet, not their seats. And there is that agenda. They're serious …" Pat Kenny, who was also on the panel, interjected to say that other political parties had "stolen their clothes" by adopting similar environmental policies, but Bowman continued: "They've no difficulty with that. I genuinely say that. They're very serious people and I've huge regard for them, huge regard for them, and I think they have a future."